the mulch book

a guide for the family food gardener

stu campbell

Library of Congress Catalog Card Number: 73-89127

ISBN 0-88266-017-9

COPYRIGHT 1973 BY GARDEN WAY PUBLISHING CO.

DESIGNED BY CYNDY M. BRADY

PRINTED IN THE UNITED STATES

To Cricket

May she not be thirty before she has a garden all her own.

ILLUSTRATED BY CATHY BAKER

contents

author's note

The Mulch Book is being prepared during a very wet summer—"the year of the great rains", as we find ourselves calling it. We have planted corn four times and it still refuses to grow with any measure of consistency. It is so wet, in fact, that to our great embarrassment here at Garden Way, we are unable to *till*, to say nothing of plant, one of our model gardens. It is hard to imagine a worse year for doing research on mulching.

Much of the material in *The Mulch Book* has been gathered from sources other than our own direct in-the-garden research. To do or to redo all of the actual controlled experimentation that would allow me to make some of the statements I have made here with complete authority, would take many years. We think that a mulching book should be made available to you before that much time has passed. So I am grateful to all of the capable gardening researchers and writers I have quoted herein (if I have misquoted them somehow, that has never been my intention), and to all others who have perhaps not been quoted directly but have influenced my thinking.

I feel particularly indebted to Robert Rodale and to the editors of the Rodale Press in Emmaus, Pennsylvania who I cite frequently. All of us here at Garden Way are deeply grateful to these pioneers in, and spokesmen for, the extremely important "organic gardening" movement that is taking place in the United States and throughout the world now.

At the same time we find it a little embarrassing and unfortunate that we are so often identified with the organic gardening school as expressed by the Rodale Press, which publishes, among other things, *Organic Gardening and Farming.*

Contrary to what lots of people seem to believe about us, we are not strict proponents of organic gardening *per se*. Nor are we opponents. We just have a few reservations. To anyone willing to listen to us, we cannot emphasize enough the importance and value of building organic matter into the soil. On this point we are in complete agreement with the Rodale people. At times though, we find ourselves objecting to their rigidly-defined approach to gardening, to some of their literature and to some of their conclusions.

We also are desperately concerned for the environment, but our primary interest at the moment is in promoting *successful* gardens. If pesticides and insecticides carefully selected and used by an intelligent and cautious home gardener are going to help him save his plants from infestation and achieve this end, then we think that he, if anyone, should use them. In fact, we believe that the small-scale food grower is far more capable of using such things safely than are members of agribusiness who are apt to dump tons of harmful chemicals on their land without thought about the long-range consequences. Garden Way does not, of course, know all the answers, but please don't assume, because of "Rodale et al" footnotes, that we are not sometimes conscientious objectors to the purely Rodale way of seeing things.

preface

(unrequired reading)

Mulching first began to appeal to me when I realized that it might save me and my family some work. You see, I detest hand weeding. That may be an admission that any so-called "gardener" should never make. I think it is because I had to do so much of it in my mother's large garden as a boy. My father wasn't about to do any. If I am honest with myself—which I try to be only on rare occasions—I realize that I actually did very little weeding and a great deal of complaining about it. Because *I* justifiably could not be trusted to, my mother did all of the interesting stuff like planting, staking and picking. The hot, repetitious gnome's work was relegated to me. And you know: an amazingly large number of my friends who are still turned off about gardening have similar horrifying memories—however accurate or inaccurate they may be—of acres and acres of witchgrass to be pulled; row upon row of corn to be cultivated.

Whether or not mulching actually *does* save you work—when you consider the number of calories expended to build a garden as compared to the number of calories you take out of it—has never been accurately documented so far as I know. But I like to think that it does. It *surely* saves you a lot of time which you would have had to spend cultivating and weeding. In fact the very nicest thing about mulching when you come right down to it, is that if you mulch, your *children* may not have to do so much monotonous work in the garden. And this leads me to the very first point of *The Mulch Book:* even if *we* were, *we can not allow our children to be turned off by gardening.* Don't children learn more if their drudgery is reduced? It is they, after all, who must learn—and teach their children—to grow food for themselves, to make use of materials sparingly and wisely, and to give back to the precious land at least some, if not all, of what they take from it.

I feel in my own case that I should try to keep history from repeating itself. But in spite of my efforts to make gardening less work for my family by mulching, I am as guilty as the next parent when it comes to turning my children off. Our three-year-old daughter comes wandering into the garden when I am there, overflowing with questions, eager to explore, bursting with helpfulness. My delight at seeing her there nearly mirrors the fascination in her eyes. But soon I am preoccupied and slightly impatient with her persistent questions. I answer her inadequately—something I vowed at the moment of her birth that I would never do. I worry about her stepping on things. I am anguished that her stubby fingers can't spread carrot seeds evenly enough. When she picks leaf lettuce she accidentally pulls up the plant by the roots instead of pinching off the leaves the way she has been told. I correct her, and she must see something different in my face or hear something different in my voice because *her* expression changes. She is of course too little to understand that I act this way because of the frequent lapses in the gardening confidence which *I* still have. So she drifts sadly away to find something or someone more interesting. I worry that the garden has lost her.

So the second point is this: after months of studying the intricacies of mulching, the temptation is to think of mulch as the panacea for all gardening ills. *It is not.* As one old gardener cautioned me, mulching is just one arrow in the gardener's quiver. All of us—gardeners as well as the other unfortunate non-gardening individuals who also happen to inhabit our planet—have to retain a sense of perspective. Gardening is like anything else. We can get so bogged down with "the way we've always done it", that we never permit the gardening part of ourselves to grow in the same way we hope our gardens will. On the other hand it is the wise and confident gardener who knows enough to guard against fads. Instead of scurrying off to buy and try the "newest and latest" thing, he takes a long, closer look to see if it will, in fact, benefit him in *his* particular situation.

I want you to remember— all the time you are reading *The Mulch Book*— that mulching is only a *part* of gardening. It is not the whole story. *The Mulch Book* is only one brief chapter in the tremendous body of scientific information, practical experience, literature and folklore which comprises the *"Complete Gardening Book"*, which because of its vast nature, can never be fully written.

In the final analysis—to anticipate the book a little for you before you even begin—mulching is like a double-headed axe. It is a useful tool, but it can be a dangerous one if not used carefully. In most cases, mulching should be used like an insurance policy, as a way of hedging your bet on the success of your garden. Ideally we should have large enough gardens, all of us, so that we could mulch part of each crop—guarding it against drought, weeds, and heat—and leave the other part without mulch. By not going whole hog, either way, in any given year, we would all at least come up with something to eat.

Charlotte, Vermont   *Fall 1973*

[*1*]

here's why (very quickly)

Have you ever become annoyed with the author of a how-to book because he spent so much time explaining *why* you should be doing whatever it is he thinks you should be doing, that he has left himself little time and space to explain *how*? I'll try to resist falling into that trap here.

It seems, though, that mulching does deserve some kind of justification. For one thing, "mulch" doesn't even *sound* very nice, which may be one strike against it to begin with. In its very earliest Middle English sense the word "mulsh" was an adjective which meant, according to Mr. Webster, "soft or yielding". That's not so bad. But by the time our language had evolved into what is now called Early Modern English centuries later, the "s" in *mulsh* had become a "c", the adjective had become a noun, the word itself had come to mean "rotten hay", and something pleasant was lost in the evolution.

Now this is not to suggest that "rotten hay" is *necessarily* undesirable nor that rotted hay is the only kind of mulch there is. There are many, many kinds of materials that can be used for mulching, as we shall see. In fact, if you use your imagination a bit you probably can

There are still plenty of "model" gardens around, with arrow-straight rows and bare, immaculately-cultivated earth. This is fine if you have lots of time, even more patience, and a few slave laborers around your house.

dream up some things to use for mulch which are not mentioned in this *Mulch Book*. The point is that to the layman the thought of hoarding, handling and spreading around heaps of old, dark, moldy hay at best is "strange", not to say repulsive. To the knowledgeable gardener, on the other hand, mulch can be the most beautiful stuff in the world.

But mulching needs justification among serious and experienced gardeners too. It is awfully hard to imagine at first glance that a subject like mulching could be very controversial. I mean, either you like to mulch your garden or you don't, right? Not so. Highly regarded gardening authorities like Ruth Stout (known to many gardeners as the "complete mulcher") and Leonard Wickenden, a prominent bio-chemist and thoroughly experienced organic gardener, have carried on a mulching debate in gardening literature for years. Some people don't know with whom to side, so they don't bother to mulch at all. We'll have a look at each of their points of view a little later on.

Some object to mulching for purely esthetic reasons. Lots of gardeners prefer the traditional look of arrow-straight rows and bare, immaculately-cultivated earth. There still are plenty of these "model" gardens around, and that sort of thing is fine if you have lots of time, even more patience, and maybe a few slave laborers around your house who can help you maintain this kind of elegance. Most of us do not. Let's face it, except for the very affluent, the days of the full-time hired gardener are gone forever. Besides, mulch does not *have* to be unattractive, as we shall see also.

Here at Garden Way in Charlotte, Vermont we have a frost-free growing season that is only a hundred and forty days long on the average. We type-cast ourselves as "relaxed gardeners." Working in our test gardens, under the critical eye of our master gardener, Dick Raymond, we forever are seeking and researching new and easier ways of doing things. And we think that if you are a long-time gardener or just beginning, you should be considering some of the advantages of mulching.

Because we work our gardens here in a northern sector of the country, we know that what works well *specifically* for us may not necessarily work well for you in your garden. You also should remember that there is no one "right" way and no one "wrong" way to mulch. There are good ways and there are not-so-good ways. This book offers suggestions about *some* ways to mulch your vegetables, berries and fruits to make them tastier, healthier and more nourishing. It will try to make you aware of certain dangers and pitfalls, but it will never say, "This is *the* way." That is for you to decide.

Mulching has many benefits, not the least of which —as far as I'm concerned—is that you can walk around in your own garden on rainy days and not have three inches of sticky mud on the soles of your shoes when you come back inside. I choose to ignore the experts' warnings about staying out of the garden on wet days. I *do* try not to touch anything—mindful that I *might* be transmitting some harmful bacteria or viruses to the plants. I try to stay in the middle of a mulched path so I don't compact the soil near my plants. But it seems to be a compulsive ritual with me that I go into my garden at least once a day, squat down next to a row, and gently—sometimes not so gently—try to coax young seedlings into growing faster, bigger or greener. Without mulch this would be impossible. A silly argument, you say? But did you know:

1. Mulching does NOT significantly affect the acidity or alkalinity of your soil. Studies show that any number of organic mulching materials can be used in the vegetable garden without lowering *or* raising the pH of the soil. It's probably not necessary to worry—as most mulchers have at one time or another—about oak leaves or sawdust, for example, "souring" your soil. In fact, active continuous mulching with different materials eventually will *neutralize* the pH in almost any soil.[1]

2. Mulch is a soil conditioner. Ordinary soil which might normally break up into chunks when it is tilled or cultivated will disintegrate into fine granules after it has been mulched even for as short a time as several weeks. Sandy soils or clayey soils benefit most if they have organic matter added to them.

3. Organic mulch can contribute potassium to the soil. This is just one third of the reason why mulch has been called a "perpetual source of fertility". It can also contribute nitrogen, phosphorous and trace elements. In other words, mulch *is* fertilizer. (See Chapter Three, #7.)

4. Mulches fertilize over a longer period of time than chemical fertilizers. Organic mulches decay toward the bottom where they come in contact with the soil. This benefits the soil, not only through the release of nutrients over an extended period of time, but adds materials to the soil that help to make the soil crumbly.[2]

5. Mulching practically eliminates all weeding and cultivating. When weed seeds germinate and begin to

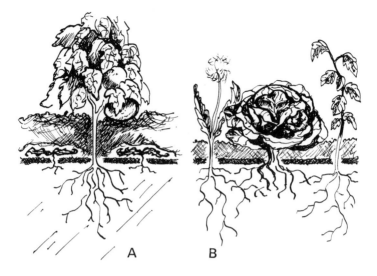

If the mulch is deep enough (A) weeds will come up in darkness and wither away. If a mulch is too thin (B) some weeds will poke themselves through. Even when this is the case they are easy to spot and easy to pull.

come up under mulch they come up in darkness and wither away. Those that do have the fortitude to poke themselves through are easy to spot and even more easily plucked. Any area that is mulched heavily needs no cultivating. (See chapter Three, #1.)

6. Mulch protects ripened vegetables. Ripe tomatoes, peppers, melons, squash and pumpkins—just to name a few—need never come in direct contact with the soil if there is mulch. This means fewer "bad" spots, fewer rotten places, and less mold.

7. Mulching encourages the presence of earthworms. Earthworms aerate the soil and release nutrients in the form of "castings". Earthworms should be considered prominent citizens in any garden and are particularly important in perennial beds or in garden plots which are never plowed or tilled.

8. Mulch protects plants from raindrops. From raindrops you say! Have you ever seen a slow-motion film or a photograph of the damage a single raindrop can do to your soil during a pelting storm? Energy from falling raindrops is dissipated on mulch. Mulch acts as a buffer zone to protect your soil from splash damage and keep fruit clean.

Raindrops can do a lot of damage in your garden during a pelting storm. Not only is the soil disturbed, but mud is splashed onto your vegetables.

9. Mulch helps your soil retain moisture. This is mulch's most universally-recognized virtue. Authorities and test results differ, but it is clear that moisture evaporation from the soil is reduced anywhere from ten to fifty percent under mulch. Mulch keeps the soil from drying out because it prevents *dew* and water drawn up from the subsoil from escaping. (See Chapter Three, #5, #8.)

Contrary to what a lot of people believe, dew is not only condensation of water from the atmosphere, but is condensation of moisture from the air in the *soil*. Most dew is a complete waste as far as plant growth is

Mulch keeps the soil from drying out because it inhibits evaporation of dew and moisture which is drawn up from the subsoil by capillary action.

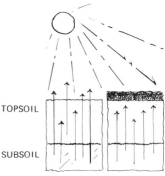

TOPSOIL

SUBSOIL

concerned—unless there is something on the surface to catch it and prevent it from evaporating.[3] Impervious mulches like polyethylene, tar paper, aluminum foil, or even old boards can catch more dew than other mulches because little air or moisture can pass through.

10. Mulch stimulates increased microbiotic activity in the soil. Certain bacteria are every bit as important as worms. The result of their work is that organic matter breaks down more rapidly and plant nutrients are made available to your plants sooner. This means, as Ruth Stout suggests, that your garden is operating very much like a compost heap, and that the compost-pile process of building humus for your garden could be skipped.

11. Mulches are environmentally safe. Whether you choose to accept the environmentalists' alarming arguments or not, we have no *choice* but to become more environmentally conscious. Mulches are every bit as effective for weed control as powerful herbicides. With organic mulches no harmful poisons like those contained in some sprays and dustings are leached into the water supplies of people and animals. Mulching reduces—and ultimately eliminates—the need for chemical fertilizers which benefit your soil only temporarily, and can burn your plants in the process. *Pure* organic gardening may be both impractical and impossible, (what you use for mulch may have been grown with chemical fertilizers, for instance) but steps in that direction often make lots of sense.

12. Mulching reduces the need for root pruning young shrubs and trees. This is just another of the many ways mulching saves you work. Because mulch helps retain moisture in the soil around newly transplanted trees, bushes and shrubs, recently traumatized roots don't have to compete with each other so fiercely for moisture and nourishment.

13. Mulching prevents soil compaction. Water penetrates through loose, granulated soil, but runs off

Mulch controls erosion by slowing water runoff and holding soil in place.

hard, compacted earth. Mulching *keeps* your soil friable without your having to work at it.

14. Mulch controls wind and water erosion. Mulch slows water runoff and helps hold soil in place —even on steep slopes. This is why we see newly grassed banks along new highways covered with mulch. Mulch keeps down dust, too.

15. Although it invites some undesirable characters, mulch discourages certain moles, cut worms, Mexican beetles, potato bugs, and other pests. Specific mulches, as we shall see, keep out a host of other unwanted guests. (See Chapter Three #2 and #6.)

16. Mulched plants are less diseased, healthier and more uniform. There is much evidence that mulching directly reduces plant disease.[4] One reason is that mulching prevents fruits and plants from being splashed, and reduces losses of plants from diseases the soil might harbor. Fit plants, like fit animals, resist sickness and not only survive, but thrive. If they are better fed and are afforded better protection, they become better specimens. As many gardeners have said so often: healthy strong plants tend to be bothered less by insects and other pests. (See Chapter Three #1 and #9.)

17. Mulches improve and stabilize soil structure. Adding organic matter to your soil through mulch causes the soil particles to be distributed more evenly throughout the upper layers of your earth. This is, after all, where you do most of your gardening. Because beneficial biological activity can take place *closer* to the surface under mulch, the soil there becomes darker and richer sooner.

18. Mulch is an effective controller of some nematodes and root knot. Experimenters at the University of Florida Agricultural Experiment Station used mulch with tomatoes, peppers, eggplant, squash, cantaloupes, watermelons, beans, celery and lettuce. Their report said, "Rotting vegetable matter piled around the plants have a very marked effect in checking the development of root knot and in enabling the plants to withstand . . . disease."[5]

19. Mulch stabilizes soil temperature. Most simply stated: mulch is insulation. It acts just the way insulation works in your house. It keeps the soil around your plants' roots cooler during hot days and warmer during cooler nights. Some mulches have higher insulation value than others. Jerry Baker, the popular gardening expert, is right in this respect. Plants *are* like people in that they are uncomfortable, even endangered by extreme fluxuations in temperature.

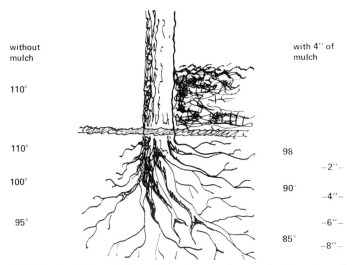

Mulch is insulation. It keeps the soil around your plants' roots cooler during hot days and warmer during cooler nights. The roots of a newly transplanted raspberry cane, for example, will die on a very hot day if the soil temperature is allowed to rise much above 100 degrees F.

9   *here's why (very quickly)*

20. Mulching reduces household waste and eliminates garden waste. Even if you live on a quarter acre of land and have a tiny garden, you generate tremendous amounts of waste in and around your home and in your garden. Much trash is organic matter and can be shredded or chopped and used as mulch. Kitchen refuse is incredibly valuable as a side dressing (In fact, I think it would be great if people could rig a drainage line from the garbage disposer directly to the garden or compost pile, instead of into a sewer or septic system where its value is lost).

Even a small plot of land can produce literally *tons* of valuable organic matter each year. Don't burn it or throw it away. USE IT UP! Dead plants, leaves and grass clippings can and should be recycled directly back into your garden. By mulching we can produce a lot more of what we consume and *consume a lot more of what we produce.*

The hardest thing about mulching, believe it or not, is putting it down in the first place. (In fact, once you get into mulching you may discover that you can have a much *smaller* garden and produce just as much as you did before). Once the mulch is down, you can relax and let nature take its course. Maybe—so that you feel that you are doing *something*—you will want to wander into the garden once in a while to give your plants a little verbal encouragement. Other than that forget the weeding, forget the watering, digging and cultivating.

More and more gardeners are joining the fraternity of "relaxed gardeners", and are enjoying both better gardens and more time to accomplish other productive things around the home. They are no longer asking themselves, "*Should* I mulch?" Now the questions are: "To what *extent* do I mulch?" "*When* do I mulch?" "*How* is mulch going to benefit this particular plant?" and "How *much* do I use?"

[2]

what are we talking about?

I find that good gardeners—probably because they like to *garden* more than they like to study about the technicalities of gardening—use gardening terms rather loosely. Ask ten gardeners to define a word like "mulch" or a word like "compost" and you will get the proverbial ten different answers. Interestingly enough, in the particular case of these two words (compost and mulch), you might find that the varying definitions not only are confused, but frequently overlap and are sometimes reversed.

Here seems as good a place as any to explain what we at Garden Way mean when we use some of the terms that already have been mentioned in Chapter One. These are not meant to be strict, inflexible defintions. In fact, you may disagree with them totally. They are offered simply as *working* definitions to describe what *I* mean when I use a particular word. Let's start with "compost."

Compost is organic matter which is undergoing or has resulted from a heat-fermentation process. This heating, generated by intense bacterial activity, may develop temperatures as high as one hundred fifty or one hundred sixty degrees Farenheit near the center of the compost pile. Heat is the distinguishing factor separating compost and mulch. In other words, if the material has not heated, it is not compost.

Sheet composting is a term we use frequently because all of *our* test gardens are built by and designed to accommodate roto-tillers, which we use constantly. "Sheet" composting actually is more akin to mulching than it is to composting. It is an efficient way to rapidly build up the organic content in the soil. A layer of organic matter (leaves for example) is laid on the top of the growing surface and then worked into the earth by a plow, a roto-tiller or spade. Once it is covered or partially covered with dirt, the organic matter decomposes very rapidly, but without heat. The end result of all composting is humus.

Humus is dark, rich, well-decomposed organic material. When the top soil in a garden contains a generous amount of humus, the garden probably is a fertile, productive one. Rotting organic matter cannot be considered humus until you no longer can identify what the original compost material was. Humus can result from decomposing mulch as well as from compost.

Mulch might be defined as unfinished, unheated compost. It can be *described* as any material which is applied to the surface of the soil to act as a barrier to retain moisture, to insulate, to feed and protect plants, or to fertilize and stabilize the soil structure. A properly functioning mulch should have two basic properties: (1) It should be light and open enough to permit the passage of water and air, while at the same time (2) be heavy enough to inhibit or even to choke off the growth of weeds. Mulches can be divided into two fundamental categories:

Organic mulches probably are the most desirable of the two for the non-commercial home gardener. Any biodegradable material—anything that will rot—can be used as organic mulch. Vegetable matter is preferable to something like old cedar shingles, planks or magazines and newspapers—although these *do* make effective mulches if you can stand to see them in your garden. The most common organic mulches are hay, straw, grass clippings, leaves and leaf mold, waste wood material, and by-products like ground corn cobs, spent hops from breweries and buckwheat hulls.

Artificial mulches, sometimes called "inert mulches," are those which do not have plant material at their origin. They are things that will *never* rot, such as polyethylene plastics, fiberglass and aluminum foil. Some artificial mulches are used quite successfully in some ways, even though they contribute nothing to the soil and are thus frowned upon by strict disciples of the organic gardening doctrine.

There are other terms associated with mulching which are sometimes bandied about:

Seed-free mulches are just what they imply: any organic mulch which has not yet or never will go to seed. This can include hay which has not yet blossomed. If you use a seed-free mulch there is no danger of donating potential weeds to your garden.

Feeding mulches are those that will rapidly add plant food to your soil. Rotted manures and compost (compost also *can* be used as mulch) are the most obvious kinds of feeding mulches.

Living mulches are flat, shallow-rooted ever-spreading ground cover plants like myrtle, thyme, sweet woodruff, English ivy and pachysandra. These mulch-plants are generally associated with border flower beds and rock gardens, but they can be both attractive and effective in the food-growing garden as well.

Green-growing mulches (or "green manures" as *we* sometimes call them) basically are cover crops like rye grass or buckwheat. They afford fine winter and erosion protection. They can be tilled under and thus "sheet composted," or they can be harvested and used for mulch in another part of the garden.

Stubble mulching is a technique used more on large farms than in home gardening situations. The cover crop is harvested, but instead of burying the dead res-

Cover crops like buckwheat afford fine winter and erosion protection. It can be tilled under and used as a "green manure".

idue right away, the stubble is left in place to form a mulch which protects the land.

Homemade mulches usually consist of materials that have been gleaned from household refuse. They might include dry coffee grounds or tea leaves and chopped paper. Vegetable refuse and garbage, if not tossed on the compost heap, can be thrown directly on the garden. If this somehow offends you, you can discreetly tuck it under mulch that is already there. Who's to ever know? Neighborhood dogs, incidentally, are not attracted to garbage that is buried under so much mulch that no scent can escape.

My wife's grandmother gave us one of those deluxe kitchen blenders for Christmas last year—one of those complicated-looking types with all the buttons. So now I use the old one indirectly as kind of a garden tool. I am tyrannical in my insistence that everyone in the family save every *scrap* of organic waste material—including banana peels, apple cores, carrot peelings, coffee grounds, used tea bags, even egg shells and dead flowers, along with anything else we can find. I am sure I

After the stubble mulch has done its work, it can be tilled under where it will add organic matter to the soil.

am driving everyone nuts, but I throw all of this into the blender each day, add some water and grind it up.

I even have ground up the cleanings from fish I have caught in Lake Champlain, for after all, American Indians used to plant a fish under each hill of corn, didn't they? I try to avoid doing this sort of thing when we have guests, but when there's just family around I dump this wet, chopped-up mess on my compost heap. I have been amazed how quickly it rots—the chopping vastly increases the surface area for bacteria to get at —and is assimilated into the darkness of the pile. I might better pour it directly into the garden where it might do more good still. Lots of goodness gradually is leached out of a compost heap into the soil below.

Contour mulching works very much like contour plowing. If your garden happens to be on a side hill, try laying coarse mulch in topographically level strips. This will prevent your good topsoil from washing downhill. Your strips can be laid in the early spring even before

CONTOUR MULCHING. *Terracing sidehills and mulching in level strips can prevent your good topsoil from washing downhill.*

your earliest seeds are planted. If your garden is in a slightly "rolling" place, you may discover that your level strips of mulch create an attractive, curving, terraced effect.

Dust mulch is just dirt stirred up by a hoe or cultivator. The theory behind dust mulching is that a layer of dust will discourage shallow-rooted weeds and conserve moisture by keeping the soil beneath from drying out by breaking the capillary action cycle which draws moisture upward from the subsoil. If this sounds suspiciously like a non-work-saving process, it is.

Fortunately for us "relaxed gardeners," tests show no significant differences between soils under a dust mulch and those with an undisturbed surface. Usually the act of forming such a mulch kicks up soil particles and exposes them to even more air and more sun than if they had not been disturbed. About the only good this hard work accomplishes is that it *does* kill weeds which rob the soil of moisture.[6] Descriptions of how to grow certain crops like celery call for the plants to be "dust mulched." What they describe is closer to "hilling" than it is to mulching. If you like to *cultivate*, to introduce fresh oxygen to soil levels below the surface, go ahead and cultivate. But let's not confuse cultivating with mulching.

Permanent mulches are usually made up of non-disintegrating (not necessarily nonbiodegradable) materials. Permanent mulches like crushed stone, gravel, marble chips and calcine clay particles are useful particularly in perennial beds, around fruit trees, and on soil which is not likely to be tilled or cultivated.

What are we talking about when we get ready to choose a mulch? Specific mulches, along with their particular advantages and disadvantages will be described in a separate chapter, but there are a few general things to consider:[7]

1. Cost. Mulch need not be expensive unless you are looking for a lot more than you can scavenge or for something rare or exotic.

2. Availability. This should be the number-one consideration when you are deciding what to use for a mulch. Good mulch might be more readily available than you think, and free to boot! Look around your house, garage, yard and garden. If your needs are not met there, you probably don't have to look any further than your own immediate community. Check factories, saw mills and street or park departments. Remember the old law of supply and demand. What is plentiful and available is probably cheap.

3. Weight and bulk. This affects transportation costs, of course, but more directly it affects your ability to handle the mulch easily.

4. Appearance. The appearance of a mulch is important to some; far less important to others. In any case, this is a highly personal consideration. Get a look at what you are thinking of buying, then try to visualize how it is going to look in *your* garden.

5. Water penetration. How easily does water seep through the mulch? Some inert mulches are totally waterproof.

6. Moisture retention. How effectively does the mulch prevent the soil from drying out?

7. Insulative value. Does the mulch really stabilize soil temperature during extreme weather changes?

8. Fire hazard. Are you apt to be smoking when you work in the garden? Straw and peat, for instance, ignite very easily. Other materials, sawdust for example, sometimes are prone to smoldering fires which are the result of spontaneous combustion, especially if they are applied in a layer that is much too thick.

9. Lasting qualities. How often does the mulch need to be replenished or replaced? Fine or chopped mulches rot faster and feed plants sooner, while coarser mulches generally last longer and demand less work.

10. Wind effect. If you live on a windy hill and you decide to use paper or black plastic mulch, you'd best be sure to anchor it well with pegs, stones or other weights. Lighter organic mulches like buckwheat hulls also are not likely to stay in place in high winds.

11. Odor. Fresh manures, grass clippings and some other mulches can give off an offensive odor for a while. Some people for example object to the smell of chocolate given off by cocoa hulls.

12. Decomposition characteristics. Does the mulch used add nitrogen or does it diminish the amount of nitrogen in the soil? How do you know the soil is being robbed of nitrogen, and what can you do about it?

In all fairness, there is one last thing to be admitted. If you decide to mulch on a large scale, we may be talking about a *bit* of work for you initially. If you have been using chemical fertilizers exclusively on your garden for some time, or if you are beginning on a new plot, you may find that your garden is so deficient in organic matter that it will seem to devour any organic mulch you feed it. One lady in Wisconsin who for years complained about her garden's inability to grow anything very successfully, finally wrote to the publishers of *Organic Gardening* magazine,

Mulching took on the attributes of a nightmare. The garden opened its jaws and gulped down mulch far faster than we could provide it. When we walked down the rows of mulch it snapped, crackled and shrank. When it rained, the mulch became soft and gushy and shrank. Under the winter snow it all but disappeared.

In the spring the need for more mulch to cover the garden's nakedness was renewed. The old nightmare chugged and chased at our heels . . . We hauled in sawdust, spoiled hay, more sawdust, marsh grass, woodchips, spoiled hay. We salvaged cut grass along the roadside. Every leaf that blew in the wind was gathered and added to the mulch. Every blade of grass, every weed was pounced on for mulch . . .

After five years of mulching my temperature has finally subsided. I too lie in the couch by the window and anticipate the first head of lettuce sprouting a blue ribbon from its leaves.

The proof of its value is under the mulch. The earth is soft, moist, and full of earthworms. I had longed for a garden soil so soft that I could scoop out a trench with my hands.

Five years of intensive mulching is too much to ask: too much work and too costly. Hers was no doubt an *extreme* case of organic-matter starvation. Even so, Mrs. Anderson's ultimate results did border on the spectacular. So her testimonial is not included here to scare you off. Neither should you be discouraged by the next chapter.

[3]

to give the devils their due

It must be almost thirty years ago now, that on a chilly spring morning a lady in Connecticut who has both a very green thumb and a way with words, wandered into her garden and felt the ever-so-faint stirrings beneath her feet that only people who are attuned to such things can feel. Little did she know at that point, I would guess, that right then and there, as the seeds of three famous gardening books *(How to Have a Green Thumb Without an Aching Back, Gardening Without Work* and *The No-Work Garden Book)* began to germinate in the fertility of her mind, that single-handedly she was about to revive and popularize the ancient art of mulching.

She wrote,

> ... I was, as usual, trying to be patient until someone could do some plowing for me, when finally one day, I used my head. No, not for plowing—for reasoning. My asparagus was doing beautifully and I said to myself: that ground hasn't been plowed for over ten years; what has asparagus got that peas haven't? To heck with plowing! I'm going to plant ...[8]

She started with the original mulch: hay—lots of it. Later Ruth Stout was to say,

This experiment, made at Garden Way years ago, verified Ruth Stout's theories about mulch on top of sod. Thick books of hay were laid on a plot of grass in the fall. In the spring plantings could be—and were—made there. The soil was moist and soft, and needed only to be scuffed with a hoe and rake. No plowing or tilling had to be done.

. . . After putting hay all over the garden I soon found that the only jobs left were planting, thinning, and picking. Whenever I wanted to put in some seeds, I raked the mulch back and planted, and later, when the seeds had sprouted, I pulled the mulch close around the little plants, thus keeping them moist and outwitting the weeds . . .

. . . My plot has become so rich now that I can plant very closely, and I don't even use manure or [chemical] fertilizer. The garden is one-eighth its original size and so luxuriant that in the fall we call it the jungle . . .[9]

The Stout complete-mulching system is very simple. She is really a sheet-composter who uses no machinery. "Make your garden your compost pile," she says.[10] "My way is simply to keep a thick mulch of any vegetable matter that rots on both my garden and flower garden all year round." A compost heap is too much trouble, she says. Just spread mulch where you eventually would have spread the compost anyway. In time it will rot and become rich dirt. In fact, she would go so far as to say that if you were to cover *sod* with a heavy layer of mulch in the fall, you could make plantings there—without plowing, tilling, or spading of any kind—the following spring.

> For the past twenty-six years I have used no fertilizer of any kind on any part of my garden except rotting mulch and cotton seed meal. I broadcast the latter in the winter at the rate of five pounds to every one hundred square feet of my plot. I'm not really convinced that my soil needs the meal, but I have been told it does for nitrogen.
>
> However, if gardeners weren't driving in here quite often to inspect my system, I think I would skip the cottonseed meal for a season and see if it made any difference. But as long as I am exhibiting the excellent results which I get from my method, with so little work, I can't afford to have a failure.[11]

Ruth Stout represents a charming antithesis to the kind of quasi-scientific approach to vegetable gardening that spewed reams of complicated, pamphletized data and contradictory advice from various headquarters of state university extension services throughout the country during the late Forties and Fifties.

She often leaves herself wide open to the criticism that she oversimplifies. Perhaps she does, but her reassuring advice to the neophyte gardener who is faced with the apparent complexities of mulching would be: *don't worry about it!* What about hay seeds in the mulch you ask? If the mulch is thick enough, she would answer, the weeds won't come through. When do you start mulching then, you might counter? *"Any* time!"

Along came Leonard Wickenden, the "gardener's organic gardener," who didn't buy Ruth Stout's act. In his encyclopedic, *Gardening With Nature,* where he relies heavily on his own scientific background, on his immense horticultural experiences, *and* on his own intuitive organic gardening sense, he jumps on mulching with both feet. He writes, in only slightly-veiled reference to Mrs. Stout:

Here we have a practice that has gained greatly in popularity in recent years . . . The soil between rows of crops is covered with a layer of straw, coarse hay, sawdust or trash of some kind. It is claimed for this practice that it retains moisture by checking evaporation, keeps down weeds, prevents undue baking of the soil and encourages the growth of earthworms. There is much truth in these claims. Weeds are by no means entirely eliminated, but those that make their way through the mulch are easily uprooted. Evaporation is checked and the soil kept cool, which means that earthworms will remain nearer the surface, although it does not necessarily follow that their numbers will increase.

But there is another side of the picture. *If soil is covered by let us say coarse hay, much of any rain that falls on it will be held by the hay.* Since this rain will be spread in a thin film over the fibers, it will evaporate readily and the soil below will never get the benefit of it. In other words, whatever may be gained by retaining moisture already in the ground may be counterbalanced by what is lost in the subsequent rainfall.

It is also a question whether the protection of the soil is entirely beneficial. Certainly in the spring every gardener longs for the warm sunshine to raise the temperature of his soil and so speed up the growth of his seedlings. *At what point do we decide the soil is getting too much warmth?*

Finally, *there is the danger that natural forces and conditions will start converting the mulch into sheet compost; . . . this is likely to rob the soil of nitrogen.* It is particularly likely to occur in a wet season when both the mulch and soil in contact with it are continuously damp and thus favorable to the growth of microorganisms.

Mr. Wickenden concludes,

. . . The advantages and disadvantages of mulching depend on the climate of the location and the weather of the season. If a mulch could be applied at the beginning of a dry spell and removed at the beginning of a wet one, its value could probably be great. Since that is impracticable there is no clear indication of its value and the matter becomes one of personal judgement.[12]

Ruth Stout counters in *Gardening Without Work*, remarking, "He [Leonard Wickenden] admits that he had never mulched his garden, yet he goes bravely ahead and explains what's 'wrong' with the idea." Her rebuttal is characteristically unscientific:

He says, "Weeds are by no means entirely eliminated," which is misleading, for he certainly gives the impression that he is talking about all, or at least most weeds. The fact is that if you mulch deeply enough all weeds are eliminated except a few perennials. . .

Next Mr. Wickenden states that if a garden is mulched, light rains will do it little or no good because the moisture will be spread out in a thin film over the hay and will evaporate. Since he doesn't mulch, he must be speaking from theory only, which reminds me that according to all the known laws of physics, bumblebees can't fly, yet they keep right on at it.

. . . Mr. Wickenden also declares that the ground needs the direct sun in the spring to warm it up, but I have found this to be true only in those sections where the earliest crops are to be planted. And since you have to pull the mulch aside anyway in order to plant, it isn't extra work to push it back ahead of time and let the sun reach the soil. Of course you have to be blessed with a mind which can figure that out. . .[13]

If you have the feeling that you are not *entirely* convinced by Ruth Stout's arguments, you have plenty of company besides Leonard Wickenden. Others have raised doubts and pointed out disadvantages to mulching:

1. One group of agricultural scientists at Ohio State has written a booklet called "Mulches for Home Grounds" which would seem so discouraging to the prospective mulcher that I can't help but wonder why they bothered to write it in the first place: **"Mulches CANNOT smother large weeds,"** they say, **"Neither**

can they diminish plant disease, and with the exception of aluminum foil, cannot reduce insect attack. It cannot have any marked effect on the vitamin or mineral content of the plant material."[14] (See Chapter One, #5, #16.)

2. Rodents and insects are likely to live and overwinter in mulch. Damp mulch is an attractive breeding ground for some insects. Mice and other rodents, drawn to the mulch by the warmth and availability of seed, may decide to take up residence there during the cold winter months. Once they have exhausted the seed supply in the hay mulch protecting raspberry plants, for example, they might start gnawing on the raspberry canes themselves. Once they have chewed through to the cambian layer of the stalk, the plant of course dies. (See Chapter One, #15.)

Rodents such as field mice may take up residence in a hay mulch during the cold winter months. Once they have exhausted the seed supply there, they might start gnawing on the very plants you are trying to protect.

3. Carpenter ants and other wood-inhabiting insects may live in mulch. Forestry entomologists trying to learn if tree diseases such as Dutch elm disease can be transmitted through mulches which consist of wood by-products like wood chips, shredded bark, and sawdust, discovered that such mulches do not harbor diseases, but *do* retain some wood-eating and wood-inhabiting insects which may attack fruit trees.

4. Certain mulches pose a fire hazard. Some mulches, like sawdust, are particularly susceptible to spontaneous combustion, as I've already mentioned. A spark dropped into a peat moss mulch can cause a fire that can smolder unnoticed for hours and be very hard to extinguish. Very dry hay and wheat straw also will catch fire easily.

5. Mulching can cause damping off. "Damping off" is a malady of plant roots caused by a fungus which thrives in too moist, poorly ventilated soil. This danger is very real if plants are mulched too early in the spring. (See Chapter One, #9.)

6. Mulch invites slugs and snails. Dark, wet places like those under mulch seem to attract wet slimy creatures like snails and slugs—again if you mulch too early. These fellows can have a field day feasting on your crops. (See Chapter One, #15.)

Dark wet places under mulch attract wet slimy creatures like slugs.

7. Certain mulches do rob nitrogen from the soil. Any very fresh mulch—light-colored, unweathered sawdust or hay—will steal nitrogen from the earth during the earliest stages of its decomposition. Plants surrounded by this stuff might take on the sickly, yellowish look of nitrogen deficiency. (See Chapter One, #3.)

8. Mulch CAN prevent rain from getting to the soil. No moisture—either from above *or* below—penetrates a mulch such as roofing paper or plastic. In a light rain, what little water does accumulate on the ground may be absorbed by an organic mulch and may never reach the soil. (See Chapter One, #9.)

9. Mulch can introduce plant diseases. Sometimes undesirable organisms such as disease-causing fungi and harmful bacteria ¢an be introduced into the soil through organic mulches. (See Chapter One, #16.)

10. Mulch slows plant growth. Mulch may delay crop maturity and produce smaller yields in some cases. Heat-loving plants such as tomatoes, which are grown in mulch, may be retarded because the late spring sun does not reach the soil around the roots and warm it sufficiently.

11. Mulch can be ugly, unpleasant and difficult to handle.
Many of the varied disadvantages of mulching which have been listed here are well-founded and well-taken. Perhaps you know of some other ways mulching might handicap your garden. If you do, we would like to hear from you. But now that both sides have been presented, we also would like to get in *our* two cent's worth. Our experience and research has taught us a number of things:

First, to answer Mr. Wickenden's questions: Won't mulch prevent rain from getting to the soil?

Yes, but not in the way he suggests. Coarse hay, which he chooses as an example, is one mulch which water penetrates most easily. Water does seem to spread in a "thin film" on the fibers, but beads of water will collect rapidly and dribble through the mulch to the soil below. In fact, in this way the soil is moistened for a while *after* a light rain shower has stopped.

Matted leaves, dry-crusted peat moss or *very* finely-chopped hay spread too thickly *can* inhibit or even prevent any water penetration. Chopped leaves seem to allow more water through. Leaf mold is better still. Peat moss is less absorbent and less likely to crust if it is mixed with something else like pine needles or even with surface soil. The problem presented by any impervious artificial mulch is solved easily: poke some holes in it to let water through to the soil!

Shouldn't the soil get sunshine? I referred this question to Garden Way's microbiologist Dr. Doug Taff. He thought for a moment and said, "I don't see why. Look at a tropical rain forest. Roots and soil there *never* see sunlight." Our gardening authority, Dick Raymond, would agree.

To germinate, a seed needs sunshine for warmth, but it needn't be full strength. (We don't advocate planting most small *seeds* under heavy mulch anyway.) It is possible that sunlight on the soil could prevent some diseases from spreading, but at the same time it would reduce beneficial microbial activity. Don't forget: It is in the green leaves of plants where the action is. That is where the photosynthesis, which requires sunlight, takes place—not in the roots (although important things happen there too). Naturally all green leaves should be kept above any mulch.

At what point do we decide that the soil is getting too much heat? Soil that is overheated can cause root damage. It is conceivable that soil might get too hot under black plastic in particularly warm climate situations—although proponents of black plastic mulch *insist* that the heat from the dark surface is given off to the atmosphere above the plastic, not to the ground beneath. It is our feeling generally that most worrying about the soil overheating under organic mulch is unwarranted. Organic matter is good insulation which discourages extremes in soil temperature.

Is it good for mulch and soil to be damp continuously? Yes. You might find it somewhat moldy under there, but all indications are that this does no damage to the soil or to the plants. Damping off is not a threat to healthy, well-established plants. If damping off *is* a problem in your area, do not mulch too closely around very young plants.

By far the vast majority of my own research directly contradicts Kiplinger and his Ohio State team. And in my own garden I have proved to myself that I *can* smother even the largest weed if I use enough mulch. But this becomes an academic question. It is ten times easier just to pull the darned thing, because the soil it's growing in is so soft and moist.

Our plants here are not especially bothered by insects. A dusting of rotenone seems to solve most of our problems. We seem to have very little plant disease in our test gardens, either where we mulch or where we

Weeds that do manage to poke themselves through are easy to pull because the soil under a mulch is so soft and moist.

don't mulch. So we are content, for the moment at least, to let the agronomists fight out the disease-mulch question among themselves. As yet we have run no tests on the vitamin or mineral content of the plant material grown in mulch, but I (perhaps mistakenly) assume that better-nourished plants bear more nourishing fruit. *This* is certainly a question that screams for controlled experimentation and verification.

What about rodents? We recommend your using a seed-free mulch around raspberries, blueberries and fruit trees. Second or third cut hay—if you can get it—normally has not gone to seed and works fine. Rodents probably won't choose to live there if there is nothing to feed on.

What about insects, slugs, and snails? I have to admit that when I look into the mulch in my own garden I feel like a giant parting the trees of some mini-rain forest. The decaying, rich-smelling area there is alive with all sorts of tiny creepy-crawling insect things, most of which I cannot identify even with the help of John and Helen Philbrick's bug manual. I don't see much evidence of their doing any harm there. So I leave them to their creeping and crawling and put the mulch back where it was.

I did mulch my garden early this year—*too* early around some plants, Dick Raymond scolds—and I *have* run across a few slugs. My wife looks for them and

Snails may have a field day feasting on your mulched crops. Fortunately they have an aversion to salt.

sprinkles them with salt whenever she is salting the cabbage plants to keep cabbage worms away. The slugs squirm a bit when they are salted and if sprinkled a second time will die. We have not seen snails yet, but I am told that their distaste for salt is similar.

What about carpenter ants and wood-inhabiting insects? If these fellows worry you I suggest four things: (1) Find bark or wood-chip mulches that have been treated with chemical insecticides or that have been composted to get rid of such creatures (some municipalities do compost their chips). (2) Carefully compost the mulch yourself for several weeks before you use it. (3) Use these mulches in places where there are no woody plants nearby and don't worry about the insects, or (4) Don't use these mulches at all; use something else that you are more comfortable with.

Is there real danger of fire in mulch? Not if you don't smoke in the garden; not if you use mulches that don't burn easily; not unless it is extraordinarily dry and you don't soak your mulch occasionally with your garden hose. Otherwise, yes, there is a danger.

How do you prevent mulches from robbing nitrogen from the soil? *We* don't, really. We make sure that there is plenty of nitrogen to go around. Ruth Stout, you'll recall, fertilizes with cottonseed meal, which is rich in nitrogen. We spread alfalfa meal on the soil before we mulch, though you might consider this an expensive alternative. We are not strict dyed-in-the-wool organic gardeners, and are not above using some chemical fertilizers like calcium nitrate to bring up the nitrogen level temporarily in a spot we expect to be robbed. All organic mulches ultimately *contribute* nitrogen to the soil. Some—dried or decaying legumes particularly—always give and never take.

Can mulch introduce plant diseases? Probably, but common sense should tell you to avoid using a mulch that you know has come from soil that contains some disease-causing fungus or bacteria. If you have a mulch that is suspect, make sure that it is *thoroughly* composted before you use in on the garden. If it is too late—it is already on the garden—consult your local experts or your county extension agent. Don't be too proud to let him recommend a chemical remedy that you can use as a stop-gap measure for *this* year.

Does mulch slow plant growth and reduce yield? It can in some cases. And it also can be ugly, unpleasant and hard to handle if you use poor judgement in choosing your mulch. This is why we recommend becoming familiar with a wide range of mulching possibilities. If your mulching repertoire is such that you *usually* can choose the right place for the right mulch at the right time, you can *hasten* a crop's maturity, *increase* and *prolong* your garden's yield and at the same time enhance the attractiveness of your garden while expending a minimum of effort, time and money. This is what the next few chapters are all about.

[4]

here's how

I think that the gardening mania that is sweeping our country is one of the best things that has happened in a long time. A Gallup Survey done recently for Garden Way Research Associates shows that—would you believe it—15 *million* people in the United States who did not have a garden in 1972, planned to have one in 1973! This doesn't mean that they *did* have a garden, but it is a strong indication of how people feel.

For some of these 15 million, the urge to garden has been part of a larger aim to seek an idealistic, even primitivistic, back-to-the-land way of life. Other more pragmatic souls who see inflated food prices as a national emergency, have renewed and modified the Victory Garden attitudes of the early Nineteen-Forties. Still others see gardening as both a way of supplementing incomes and of intensifying a sense of family solidarity and self-sufficiency at a time when such things seem to be disappearing.

One of the best short-cuts to having a self-contained, self-supporting home—an ideal situation which can never *really* be achieved—is learning to use whatever human and material resources already are there. Learning to mulch effectively, believe it or not, is a good place to begin.

Being more self-sufficient does not mean—as some people seem to think—that you have to live like Robinson Crusoe. Neighbors themselves are every bit as important as the materials, goods and services they can supply. It doesn't mean that you have to reject technology and go back to cutting your grass with a scythe because you don't have an oil well and a refinery to supply yourself with gasoline to run your rotary lawn mower.

Let's be practical. Small, efficient power tools and machines are no longer luxury items for the homeowner-gardener. They are necessities. The rotary tiller—particularly the type with tines mounted in the rear—is a work-saver of monumental proportions. It is a sheet composting machine as well as a tiller, cultivator, and furrower.

A chopper-shredder is another valuable machine for the serious mulching-gardener. It lets you make valuable mulch out of all sorts of unexpected materials and helps you make *better* mulch out of materials you already have or can get. Both machines are expensive. There is no denying that. But maybe *shared* machinery is one answer to the energy crisis and high cost of living. If you can get a neighbor or two tuned into this way of thinking you might be able to buy a tiller or a chopper (or both) together and share the cost. Who knows? Maybe later you will rent the machinery out. I understand that the going rate for roto-tilling is right around ten dollars an hour. That's not bad. You can pay for a machine pretty quickly at that rate.

While you are giving that some thought, here are a few practical suggestions for general mulching:

—Don't try to stretch your mulch too far. It's like trying to paint with a dry brush. The end result isn't worth much. Try to figure out beforehand how much mulch you are going to need. For example: It takes five to seven bushels of sawdust to mulch one inch deep on one hundred square feet of garden space.[15] Then, as Ruth Stout suggests, get about twice that much. Almost invariably you will end up using more than you

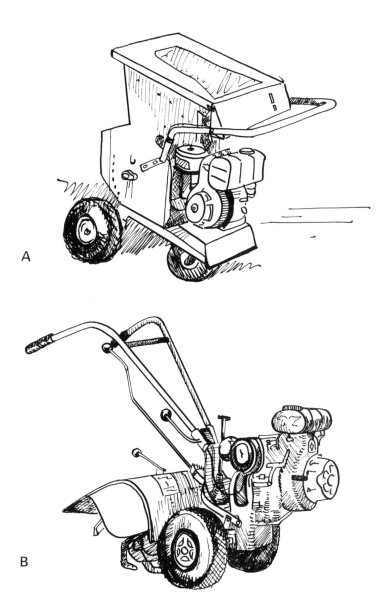

A *chopper-shredder (A) is a valuable machine for the serious mulching gardener. It helps you make mulch out of all sorts of unexpected things and lets you make better mulch out of materials you already have.*

The rotary tiller—particularly the type with the tines mounted in the rear (B)—is a sheet composter, a cultivator, and a furrower, as well as a tiller. It is a work saver of monumental proportions.

thought you would. You can always stockpile what you don't use right away.

—Always try to remember that bacteria and earthworms are strong allies for any gardener. Without help from lots of microbes in the ground, mulch would never decompose, and the vital elements that are tied up in organic matter would never get released. At Garden Way we place a lot of emphasis on earthworm activity too. [16] They "pre-digest" matter in the soil and liberate chemicals in their castings that plants can use for nourishment. Dick Raymond often has said, "If the worms won't eat it, you should think twice about using it in your garden as mulch." *Continuous* mulching is a very good practice because it keeps the worms and bacteria in business by keeping them supplied with the organic raw material they need to do their work.

—Remember too that earthworms are affected by changes in season and temperature. They are least active during the hottest months and during the coldest months. In the summer they can be coaxed into working harder if you keep enough mulch on the garden to keep the soil moist and cool. In the late fall earthworms need to be protected from freezing. This is why we recommend mulching *annual* beds for winter—(but not perennial beds; see page 55)—before the ground is frozen hard.

—Be alert for signs of nitrogen deficiency when you use certain mulches (see the Garden Way mulch chart for a complete list of which ones). Some organic mulches, such as fresh sawdust, wood chips, ground corn cobs and some cereal straws, can cause a depletion in soil nitrogen. Because the bacteria which are breaking down the mulch and turning it into humus require such a large amount of nitrogen themselves, they take it from the nitrogen source most available to them, from the soil. This, as I have already suggested, makes the plants look yellow and stunted, because they are not getting enough nitrogen themselves.

—Fertilizer should be applied at the first signs of yellowing. You can stave off nitrogen starvation with a side dressing of sodium nitrate (which we used to call nitrate of soda), calcium nitrate or a complete fertilizer which is high in nitrogen, such as 10-6-4. Mix any of these with water if you like. Mulch is no hindrance to a fertilizer-in-water solution. You even can apply the fertilizer dry by stirring it down next to the soil.

What about dosage? Try this: for a two hundred square-foot area, use one pound of calcium nitrate or sodium nitrate or two pounds of complete fertilizer which has ten percent nitrogen (10-6-4).[17]

—You also can "inoculate" nitrogen-robbing mulches. That sounds very medical and very complicated, but all it means is that you mix fertilizer with a fine mulch like sawdust or ground corncobs before you use it on the garden. One half pound of sodium nitrate or calcium nitrate per bushel of mulch is about right.[18]

Our authority, Dr. Doug Taff, cautions against using ammonium nitrate as a quick nitrogen builder-upper, and suggests using calcium nitrate instead. He tells me, "Ammonium nitrate is really catching a lot of flack from people in the agribusiness. They are finding out that ammonia is really nasty stuff in the soil. It's so caustic that it actually can sterilize the ground."

—If plants under a plastic mulch show signs of needing side dressing, fertilizer can be dissolved in irrigation water and allowed to run through T-shaped slits in the plastic. The stem of the "T" should point toward the direction the water is coming from.[19]

—In general the thickness of your mulch is going to depend on the material you are using. Usually the finer the material, the thinner will be the layer. Mulch depth can vary from half an inch for something like coffee grounds to twelve inches for something like coarse straw.

—Don't forget that plant *roots* need to breathe, too. Air is one of the vital elements in any good soil structure. Soil that is too compact has little or no air. One of the benefits of mulching, as you'll recall, is that it prevents this kind of soil compaction. But don't mulch so deeply

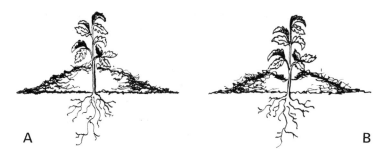

A   B

TWO WAYS TO MULCH ROW BEDS. In a rainy year, mound the mulch slightly to encourage some water to run off into the area between rows (A). If it is very dry, make a shallow furrow in the mulch along the row of plants (B). The indentation will tend to collect water which will seep through the mulch to the plants.

that you undo this good by not allowing your soil to breathe through the mulch. Wet leaves that bond together and cake, can cause this sort of air-tight problem. *Fine* mulches, unless they are applied sparingly, can prevent air penetration, too.

—Normally you will want to apply thicker mulches to sandy, gravelly soils, thinner mulches to heavy clay soil. Avoid mulching at all in low-lying spots—places that are sometimes likely to be "drowned" with water. Although it may not be necessary always, you can remove mulch during a *particularly* rainy period, if you have time, to prevent the soil from becoming waterlogged.

—Another rule of thumb: Darker mulches like buckwheat hulls and walnut shells absorb heat, and warm the soil beneath them. Lighter mulches, such as ground corn cobs, reflect light, and heat the soil less as a result. Choose mulch color according to where you live and according to the heat-loving or hardiness characteristics of the plant you are mulching.

—Heavy mulch is most effective if applied after a rain shower when the ground is moist (but not soaked). If the ground is too dry to start with, it will tend to stay dry for the rest of the summer unless there is a real cloudburst.[20]

—With most plants that are grown from small seeds, wait before applying your first mulch until after the plants are pretty well established. Mulch between the rows first, not right on top of where the seeds were planted. You can begin to mulch the seedlings just as soon as they are an inch or two higher than the thickness of the mulch you are going to use. Leave an unmulched area about six inches in diameter around each plant for about two weeks. Later, at a time when the mulch is good and dry, bring it right up to the stems.

—Do not apply wet mulches like spent hops or new grass clippings on very hot days, and be sure that they do *not* touch plant stems. When the temperature is above ninety degrees, such mulches, being wet, tend to generate so much heat that they actually can kill a plant they are in contact with.[21]

—When old mulch becomes decayed and compacted, replace it. Mulching promotes very shallow root growth. Your plants can become like a spoiled child. Because the soil stays relatively moist beneath mulch, roots do not have to grow deep and work hard, but can stay near the surface. This means that once you start mulching, you are committed to maintaining it. If you change your mind and decide to remove the mulch in midsummer, your plants may quickly die for lack of wetness.

—Fluff mulch with your hands or with a pitchfork once in a while so it doesn't get too packed down. If your mulch starts sprouting—because you have used oat straw or hay with lots of seeds or buckwheat hulls which might contain an occassional seed or two—flip the mulch upside-down on top of the unwanted seedlings to choke them off. If they persist, add more mulch to stifle them fully.

—Because weed control is one of the major benefits of mulching, you should have very little use for strong

Years ago we tried cutting holes in a roll of corrugated cardboard (A), laying it on the garden and planting corn through the holes (B). The corn grew beautifully and never needed to be weeded. But by harvest time the mulch was too soggy to till under and messy to pick up. We wondered if this wasn't more work than it was worth.

herbicides, although some people with witchgrass or other heavy weed problems mix herbicides with mulch. Do *not* try to use herbicides under plastic (and some weeds *will* grow under clear polyethylene). You will only kill your plants along with the weeds.

—Speaking of plastic, if you recognize the advantages of plastic mulch but are offended by the sight of it in your garden, cheer up. Maybe you don't *have* to look at it. The plastic—or asphalt paper for that matter—can be buried under a thin layer of something else like pine needles, crushed stone or hulls of some kind—even dirt! But I probably don't need to remind you that soil will wash right off any plastic that is laid even on a slight incline.

—Mold sometimes can and will develop in too-moist or shaded organic mulch material. You can get rid of it if you turn the mulch regularly. If it really offends you, an application of Ferbam at the rate of two pounds per one hundred gallons of water will work wonders on moldy mulch.[22] This seems like an extreme measure. In

Try separating baled hay into "books". Place rows of books between rows of plants and make yourself a place to walk on wet days.

either case mold does little harm. In fact, mold is evidence of a healthy decomposition process. It seems to offend the human eye more than it offends soil or plants.

—If you get bales of hay, try peeling off "books" or "flakes", (three or four inch layers from the end of the bale), and placing rows of books between rows of plants. This will make a clean path for you to walk on during rainy days, as well as keep the weeds down. If and when any weeds show through in force, add more layers.

"Books" tend to be pretty dense because the hay is so tightly packed by the baling machine. Sometimes it is a good idea to loosen them by pulling the hay apart a little with your hands. This is an especially good idea if you are going to throw these books on top of onion sets or potatoes which you want to grow up through the mulch.

—It is important first to cultivate around plants that are going to be mulched late. After-the-fact mulching cannot do much good if the ground already is dried and baked hard. This little bit of cultivating shouldn't make you feel too badly, knowing that you won't have to do any more there for the rest of the season, once the mulch is in place.

—Mulch is not recommended for quick-growing plants like radishes. Normally there is not enough time for the mulch to do them any good. For the most part, plants that prefer cool, moist soil respond better to mulches than those which revel on hot sun and dry soil. There are exceptions, of course, as Chapter Seven will show. In a normal year hot-weather plants like corn and eggplant are not very happy when mulched.

—It is probably not advisable to use the same mulch on the same spot year after year, just as it is not a good idea to plant the same crop in the same place year in and year out. A good mulching may last for several seasons. When finally it does decompose, it should be replaced by something else. Plants and soil seem to like variety the way you and I do.

—Mulches are excellent places for disease spores to overwinter and multiply. Remove and burn mulching material that you know has become disease-infested. Don't till it into the soil. In order not to multiply disease possibilities, the refuse of a plant being protected by mulch should not be used as its mulch. In other words, although chopped pea vines might be an excellent feeding mulch, use them somewhere other than on new pea plants.[23]

Be a creative mulcher as well as a practical one. Experiment, read, and talk to your neighbors about it. Use your tiller and your chopper, if you have them—even your rotary lawn mower—to help you try out new materials and techniques that the "armchair experts" have not even thought of yet. It is *gardeners*—sometimes only moderately experienced ones who are not yet set in their methods—who learn most and can teach us much about gardening.

It is amazing to me how willingly and effectively gardeners exchange, modify and implement new ideas. The body of gardening knowledge is growing so fast that it is very difficult to stay on top of it all. My microbiologist friend, Doug Taff, complains that some gardening books are obsolete even before going to press.

When you come up with something new, scribble it down on paper and send it to us. We'll be more than interested to hear from you, and will be anxious to pass the information along to others. In the meantime, I hope the next chapter will answer some of your questions about when and how to mulch perennial plants.

[5]

here's how with perennials

Our business is helping people to grow food—not plants for exterior decorating. So we can agree heartily with Stanley Schueler who wrote a gardening book and called it *Gardens Are For Eating*.

I realize that making any remarks against flowers is risky, for flowers are emotional things. That probably is why we are forever encouraged to "say it" (whatever *it* is) with flowers rather than with spinach or rutabagas.

So let me say, before you get the wrong impression, that there is absolutely nothing wrong with ornamental shrubbery, there is nothing wrong with broad lawns and attractive landscaping, and there is nothing wrong with flower beds, flower boxes, or flower pots. Our test gardens are filled with marigolds, nasturtiums, geraniums and other "companion" flowers that fend off insects and—more important—add color and contrast to the traditional green of the vegetables. Most Garden Way people, at least those whom I know well, have lawns and shrubs and border flower beds just like anybody else.

It's not that we question anyone whose thing it is to trim hedges, prune trees, spread turf builder, mow acres of lawn and swear a lot at crab grass. If that is

What's wrong with the idea of ornamental vegetable gardens? Even a tiny urban lot can produce a lot of vegetables and a lot of organic mulching material.

how a man likes to relax, who are we to be critical? We just wonder. Could people be persuaded to sacrifice a part (not *all*) of their elegant green expanses, and redirect some of their energies (not *all*) toward growing things they can *eat*? What is wrong with the idea of ornamental vegetable gardens?

When I talk about perennials in this chapter, I am talking about some *food-growing* plants that live year-round—not flowers. Food-producing perennials include things like asparagus, rhubarb, and strawberries. Be forewarned that there will be no attempts to discuss the mystical subtleties of mulching roses or to offer a magical mulching formula that will make your rhododendrons less subject to chlorosis. That is not *our* thing.

I wish that this chapter could have a title like "Ten Easy Steps to Mulching Perennials" or "Mulching: a Month-by-Month Calendar." Unfortunately seasons and climates vary so much throughout the country that such an approach would be inaccurate and confusing to many people. We will have to be content with general descriptions of what to do in the Spring, Summer, Autumn and Winter.

Spring As the snow starts to melt during those first warm sunny days of spring, gardeners everywhere start champing at the bit. This is the season for restraint. Because perennial plants *already* are there, it is easy to get excited on a day with sixty-degree temperatures, and jump the gun with them. Think about other things if you can. Try to remind yourself that there aren't a lot of things to worry about in the garden itself, *just yet.* Loosen mulch where it has been crushed by snow, if you like, but don't remove it too early. Spring is a good time to scout around and see what you can scavenge in the way of mulching materials.

Early spring is the time to run tall asparagus plants through the shredder or rotary lawn mower and save the choppings for mulch to be used somewhere else on the garden. This also is the time to plow, spade or roto-till winter mulch into seedbeds where you will be planting your annual plants. Don't remulch perennials until at *least* two weeks after the average date of the last killing frost—whenever that may be where you live. Give the earth plenty of time to warm up.

By mid-April here in Vermont we are just *beginning* to remove winter mulch from the perennials. This is about three or four weeks after the snow has left our valleys. This date probably will be earlier where you are. Remember: Removing too much mulch from perennials plants too early does *not* help the soil and the roots to warm-up. It may warm it for a few hours, but after the next hard freeze and subsequent thaw (and we have plenty of those in late April and May) plants may be frost-heaved right out of the ground and die of root exposure.[24]

Move protective mulch away from plants gradually and let it lie off to the side, but within easy reach. Take off a thin layer at a time, and then wait several days before you remove the next layer. This painfully slow process gives your plants a chance to harden. Josephine Nuese says,

> Don't whip off winter protection until the soil beneath the plant has thawed out. Strong March winds and strong March sun, both dehydrating, can drain the essential moisture which the still frozen roots can't replace. Don't be misled by shallow surface thawing. If you poke down with a stick and can feel ice, leave the mulch.[25]

A   B

Alternate freezing and thawing can heave plants out of the ground causing root damage (A). Evergreen boughs anchor snow and offer fine winter protection for perennial plants.

As much as anything else, mulch should be kept on so the roots and tender shoots won't grow too *soon* and get nipped by frost. If it's possible, remove the final layer of mulch on a cloudy day, so that any young shoots which *have* started are not blasted suddenly by brilliant sunshine.[26] Once the winter mulch is off completely, leave it off for several days, even a couple of weeks, before you start to mulch again.

In the very *late* spring—that means June in northern Vermont—start mulching again, to conserve moisture and control weeds before they get a head start. This is a good time to fertilize around fruit trees and berry bushes by adding some sort of feeding mulch which will contribute humus and nourish the plants. Nitrogen-rich grass clippings usually abound at this time. Use them, but dry them first. Mulch far enough away from your fruit trees—out at least to the "drip line" (that's the outer perimeter of the tree if you are looking straight down on it)—so you can be sure your mulch is doing some good directly over the tiny feeder roots.

Summer Summer is the time when mulching should start to pay dividends. During hot spells, perennial roots should thrive in the weedless, cool moist ground under mulch. You do nothing now, except have a look every now and again and renew the mulch wherever weeds show signs of getting the upper hand. Pull any persistent weeds that keep showing up.

Be crafty about choosing materials for summer mulching. Because your perennials will not be tilled, the encouraging of earthworms into your perennial beds becomes particularly important, so that your soil gets some aeration. Avoid using mulches like sawdust, pine needles and redwood by-products because earthworms avoid *them*. A continuous mulch around thick-stemmed shrubs and trees should be a coarse heavy material which allows plenty of water through, but which is not going to decay too rapidly and will last for several years.[27] Top dress through the mulch with fertilizer whenever it seems appropriate.

One thing to look out for: There is danger of crown rot in perennials—strawberries for example—during the early summer months. If there have been especially heavy rains postpone your mulching until the soil no longer is waterlogged. Do not allow mulches like peat moss, manure, compost, spent hops, or ground corn cobs to touch the bases of your plants. Leave a mulch-free circle around the stems that are several inches in diameter. The idea here is to permit the soil to stay dry and open to the air around the immediate area of the plant.[28] Most other mulches do not present this problem.

Mulch should be maintained in a young or dwarf fruit orchard throughout the summer. An organic gardener and farmer named Chuck Pendergast reports:

> In early fruit orcharding, the practice was to let the trees go to grass. In other words, the land surrounding the trees in an orchard was not cultivated and plant life was allowed to establish itself there. Year after year, this resulted in a gradual building-up of the sod. The more time it has, the tighter sod will become. Eventually there was a conflict between the grasses covering the ground around the trees and the trees which were being deprived of necessary quantities of water. Hence the practice of keeping the land in an orchard free from growth began.
>
> The immediate results of this practice were favorable. The trees' health and yield improved . . . As it is hard to prevent cover grasses from becoming detrimental once they become established, mulching is now a widespread practice in orcharding . . . We've learned something and put it to wise use.[29]

Autumn The longer that the perennial's roots can stay at work in the fall the better—up to a point. Late mulching can prolong a plant's growing season, because it provides a buffer zone against frost. Roots will continue to grow in soil as long as there is still moisture available there. When the soil water freezes and is unavailable to roots, they stop.[30] Increase your mulch volume gradually for a while, to insulate the soil and to prevent early freezing of soil moisture.

Once the frost *has* been on the pumpkin more than a couple of times, your plants probably should be given a hardening-off period similar to the one you gave them in the spring. Remove the mulch until the plants obviously are dormant and the ground is frozen.

By now you should be collecting materials for winter mulching. Maybe you will want to cut evergreen boughs. They do a great job of holding snow (a superb mulch, itself incidentally) in places where it might otherwise be blown away. After harvest time, push mulch back away from fruit trees, leaving an open space around the trunks. If you anticipate a winter rodent problem in berry bushes, grapes, or dwarf fruit trees if mulched with seedy materials, don't forget that you can wrap wire mesh, hardware cloth, or plastic protectors around trunks and berry canes. If you are really concerned, or are feeling particularly vindictive because of previous experience with rodents, you always can throw a little poison grain into the mulch. That should slow them down.

Plant cover crops like rye grass or buckwheat between the rows of annual vegetables about four weeks before frost. After the first killing frost, turn all of your dead plants back into the soil or save them to be chopped or shredded. Winter rye can be planted after the first frost and will make considerable growth during the late fall and before planting time in the spring. Make sure it's annual—not perennial—rye grass. Cover crops do a good job of retaining the soil's fertilizer nutrients that might otherwise be lost through leaching.[31] They also contribute nutrients if they die, are left in place, and eventually rot.

Fall is the best time to make use of your chopper by grinding up plant residues for future use as mulch. Use your roto-tiller, if you have one, for sheet composting into your garden space all the leaves you can get your hands on. Till in the summer mulch, too.

Winter   Should winter mulching of perennials be done before or after the ground is frozen? This has been a source of much controversy and confusion in mulching circles. Don't *you* be confused: Remember this chapter has to do with perennials. Mulch your *annual* plots early—before frost really has settled into the soil —so that earthworms and beneficial microorganisms can stay at work longer during the cold months.

Fall is one of the best times to use your chopper. Grind up plant residues from the garden for future use as mulch.

To make matters worse, *some* argue that a garden should be left naked and exposed for the winter, and John and Helen Philbrick have written:

> Mulch should not be left on over the winter because it prevents the beneficial action of the frost in the earth. Moisture should not be hindered from "coming and going" during the seasons of snow and ice. If protective mulch is in such a condition that it will break down during the winter and become part of the topsoil, it may be left. But the home gardener should study this subject carefully and be sure he knows exactly what he is doing and why he is doing it.

We *have* made a study of this—a cursory one at least. After asking ourselves the obvious question: "Why does Mother Nature arrange to have her trees drop their leaves, and then later see to it that a heavy blanket of snow insulates the ground even more? Is winter mulching then a bad thing?" We concluded that your garden, *particularly* your perennials, *should* have winter mulch. But there is no hurry to put it there.

Vermonters laugh unsympathetically at "down-country" people who bundle up under many layers of winter clothing in a futile effort to keep cold out and keep themselves warm. They learned generations ago to dress to keep their own body warmth *in*.

Winter mulch acts in the same way, except that it keeps winter soil *frozen*—even during thaws.

Winter moisture and frost ought to be allowed to penetrate the soil before you lay down a heavy winter mulch. Then, if the mulch keeps the frost in, the plants cannot be "heaved" out of the ground when the soil expands and contracts on alternately freezing and thawing days.[32]

Winter mulch protects perennial foliage from drying winds and too-bright winter sunshine. It prevents the absorption of heat in the spring and doesn't allow things to grow until after the last killing frost, when finally it is removed.[33] The initial question (in case you've forgotten): Should winter mulching of perennials be done before or after the ground is frozen? The answer: After.

Last question: How much winter mulch is enough? I suppose that it is possible to smother perennials under *too* much winter mulch. One approach to the problem might be to find out from your local bureau of the United States Weather Service the average frost depth in your area. Then roughly estimate how deep your plants' roots are. Once you know this, you might find that Dr. D. E. Pfeiffer provides a clue. He says:

> Winter mulch does the same thing that snow does: it insulates the soil to the same depth as the height of the mulch. If there is a three foot snowfall, the effect of the snow reaches down to a depth of three feet. A mulch acts in the same way . . .[34]

This doesn't mean that you have to mulch to a level equivalent to the bottom of the frost level. That would mean as much as four feet of mulch in Vermont! It only means that you should mulch to a height which is a little bit greater than your perennial plants roots are deep—that is *if* the frost level where you live goes below that point.

Here are some suggestions for mulching some of the most commonly-raised food-growing perennials.

Asparagus If you are just starting a new asparagus bed, mulching probably is not necessary at all until the second spring—although if you live in a cold place like Vermont or Minnesota, you will want to mulch for winter protection even the first year. Hay, leaves, straw, salt hay, old manure or compost are just a few mulches which are excellent for winter protection on asparagus.

The asparagus tips will come right up through the mulch whenever they are ready.

As you know, once a bed has established itself, it will continue to produce asparagus for many years. In the spring, there is no need to remove winter mulch. The tips will come right up through the mulch whenever they are ready. Eight inches of hay mulch is not too much for asparagus. Its primary purpose is for weed control, but there can be other fringe benefits:

The people at the Rodale Press make this suggestion: Try dividing your bed into two parts in the spring. Mulch half of the bed heavily with a fine material such as cocoa bean shells, ground corn cobs, chopped leaves or leaf mold. Leave the other half unmulched until shoots begin to break through the mulched half. Then mulch where you did not before. This technique should extend the asparagus season, because the unmulched part of the bed will begin to bear one or two weeks earlier than the mulched part.

Blueberries Mulching blueberries can be a tricky thing. Some argue that they should not be mulched at all unless there is good soil drainage, saying, "Although mulching may prevent some bacterial and fungus diseases, over-mulching could open a Pandora's Box of problems, particularly if the soil is poorly drained, making blueberries more susceptible to disease."[35] Other authorities admit that blueberries are apt to ripen later if they are mulched, but claim that higher yield is the end result. In fact they maintain that "larger, more fibrous root systems" will develop beneath a mulch like sawdust.[36]

Blueberries can stand a permanent mulch—anywhere from four to eight inches—of pine needles. They should never need lime.

This particular example resurrects the old myth about sawdust mulch "souring" the soil. Sawdust, as we've already seen, actually tends to influence soil pH very little in most cases, but even if it *were* to make soil more acidic, this would not hurt blueberries. They seem to do best in a soil with a pH of 4.5 to 5.0. So they never should need lime. This means that they can stand a permanent mulch—anywhere from four to eight inches—of pine needles, peat moss, oak leaves, beech leaves or other mulch that releases an acid seepage. Black plastic, neither sweet nor sour, works well on blueberries too.

Dwarf or young fruit trees I'd better let Lawrence Southwick, our Garden Way expert on dwarf fruit trees, handle this one. He writes,

A circular area of about four feet in diameter around each tree should be kept free of weeds. Mulching this area to a depth of two to six inches with lawn clippings, granulated peat moss, hay, straw or sawdust is an excellent practice. This organic matter insulates the soil against wide temperature changes, lessens heaving damage due to alternate freezing and thawing of the soil surface, maintains an even moisture supply and provides fertility. Surface mulching is very effective in making the productive top inches of soil a better feeding area for tree roots. It also entices mice, so leave a space free of mulch for several inches around the trunks. If there are signs that the rodents are gnawing the trunks, lay poison for them, or protect the trunks with hardware cloth . . .

With dwarf fruit trees in particular, the use of hay mulch under the trees in the fall will greatly lessen the bruising damage of fruits that drop off prior to picking. Materials other than hay may be used, the main consideration being that the material have a certain amount of "give" to absorb or cushion the impact of the falling fruit successfully.[37]

Straw and hay may not appeal to you because they break down relatively fast and have to be replenished. Woody mulches or coarsely-ground corn cobs, which will last anywhere from three to five years, may involve less work.[38] If you decide to use these longer-lasting mulches, don't forget that your trees still should be fertilized once a year or so. You may also want to lay something soft under the branches as harvest gets closer.

Grapes *The Organic Way to Mulching* says, "Grapes deserve mulching, even the first year. Alfalfa hay and sand-straw-steer manure mixture rank high on the list of mulch-fertilizer combinations. Before the rainy season is the best time for the overall spread of mulches and various manures. If you choose hay or shredded leaves, work additional nutriment into the soil."[39]

Raspberries Raspberries should be mulched immediately after transplanting. We use chopped hay or chopped leaves, or a combination of the two. Others use sawdust, woodchips, shavings, dried chopped cornstalks, and poultry litter. Mulch right to the canes. Dick

You may want to lay some soft mulch under the branches of your fruit trees as harvest time gets closer. It will keep your "drops" from being bruised.

Raymond says that mulch sets raspberries back in the spring, and that mulch should be loosened on raspberries at that time, or even removed for a while. He also worries about mice inhabiting the mulch, so we try to use seed-free hay.

Four to six inches of mulch can be applied to the row or over the entire soil surface. For each ton of mulch about sixteen pounds of nitrogenous fertilizer may be needed to compensate for that used by the organisms in decomposition. Red raspberry suckers which arise between rows and weeds which grow in the mulch should be removed by hand.[40]

Rhubarb Again, I like this description from the Rodale book:

Thick stalks of rhubarb result from continuous heavy feeding. To keep the soil up to the standard necessary, spread a thick mulch of strawy manure over the bed after the ground freezes in the winter. In spring, rake the residue aside to allow the ground to warm and the plants to sprout. Then draw the residue, together with a thick new blanket of straw mulch up around the plants. Hay, leaves or sawdust also make excellent mulches for rhubarb.[41]

Strawberries   W. H. Thies says that organic mulching can make the difference between a successful strawberry planting and an abysmal failure. He may be over-dramatizing a little, but mulch can be very helpful. Strawberries can be mulched right after planting. Chopped hay or straw is the mulch most frequently recommended. Some like to use sawdust. Others use cotton seed hulls, corn cobs in various textures, pine needles, wood shavings and even peat moss. The most promising runners should be nudged under whatever mulch you decide to use so that daughter plants can establish themselves. The nicest thing about mulching strawberries is that the mulch keeps the fruit clean. Even if you mulch carefully, you may find that your

Strawberries can be mulched right after planting. Chopped hay or straw is the mulch most frequently recommended.

strawberry patch will need some hand weeding once there is an extensive network of plants.

Your strawberries should have about six or eight inches of protective winter mulch if you choose loose hay—less if the hay is chopped. Winter protection not only prevents heaving which breaks roots, but protects the vulnerable crown of each plant which is in real danger in temperatures below ten degrees. They should be protected this way whenever the temperature is staying below twenty degrees for any extended period of time.[42] In this part of the country this would be somewhere between Thanksgiving and the middle of December.

Chapter Seven will have a similar discussion of how certain mulches can help or hinder plantings of annual crops. In the meantime, to break things up a bit, let's examine certain mulches and some of their individual characteristics. Read on.

[6]

here's what

I hope that someday somewhere a psychologist will do a study on "The Garden as an Art Form" to find out how a person expresses himself horticulturally. How much does a person's garden reflect his own personality?

It is obvious that gardeners grow what they like to eat, and tend not to grow what they don't like. But what about the more profound things? Do sloppy-thinking literary types have poorly arranged gardens? Is a German mathematician (not to pick on German mathematicians specifically) apt to have a neat, well-regimented plot? Do people with inferiority complexes grow tall sunflowers or pole beans to compensate for their feelings of inadequacy? Or do they grow potatoes? Do ugly people grow beautiful gardens, or vice-versa? Is a weak-willed male likely to mulch with cocoa bean hulls because his *mother* always mulched with cocoa bean hulls? Does it follow that a man with a green thumb is *necessarily* a clumsy lover? Does it take a sophisticated, well-rounded, creative type to develop new gardening techniques and come up with new mulching materials? The mind boggles at the possibilities.

These are just some things to be thinking about while you're mulching or when you have nothing better to do. To be a little more serious, here is information which I hope will influence *your* mulching personality:

Aluminum Foil Aluminum foil is a relatively expensive artificial mulch. It is so artificial *looking* that many people find it unattractive. You can buy it in various widths. Normally a strip of foil is laid on the ground at planting time, and a parallel strip is laid two to four inches away from it. Plantings are made in rows between the strips. Aluminum foil is not a bad insulator, although most organic mulches are better.

Because it reflects the heat and brilliance of the sun—shooting light back up under the leaves of the plant, which helps to boost photosynthesis—aphids and other insects shy away from foil-mulched plants. Aluminum, of course will never rot and it should be taken up in the fall. If a large amount of aluminum is left in the soil for a long time there is some danger of aluminum toxicity. Foil crinkles easily and will break or tear if it is handled too frequently or if you walk on it. *Alumnized plastic,* polyethylene which has a shiny metallic coating, is a little easier to manage than aluminum foil and has many of the same advantages. One strong point in favor of the foil over the plastic: aluminum can be recycled.

Asphalt Asphalt, which most of us call tar, sometimes is used by landscape contractors to hold soil in place on steep banks while grass seed is germinating there. It disintegrates after about a year. Applying asphalt in this way is expensive and difficult, because you have to rent or buy the right equipment and know how to use it properly. It generally is impractical for the home gardener.

Asphalt paper Experiments with roofing paper here in Charlotte were discouraging because the material was so difficult to hold in place without tearing. Builders' "felt" paper, which is not so brittle, can be laid

A

B

C

ONE WAY TO LAY "FELT" PAPER MULCH. Lay strips of paper next to the row to measure spacing, and cut notches for the plants with a knife or heavy shears (A). Slide the notched paper closer to the plants (B). Then slide the edge of the unnotched strip under the other. Make sure that all edges and corners are well weighted with stones or soil (C).

with some success next to early tomato transplantings. It will absorb heat and warm the soil around the roots. Tar is toxic to some plants, so use tar paper with discretion.[43]

Bark, chopped   Bark which has been chopped by a hammer mill can be stringy and difficult to manage. Some lumber companies even go so far as to *grind* the bark material into particles of different diameters. You can get this in "all purpose," "fine grit," "pea," or "chestnut" sizes.

Bark decomposes rather slowly, but some chopped bark which is packaged and sold commercially has been composted first. This breaks down more readily. "Tan bark" which you also can buy, comes from white oak bark that has been used in a leather tanning process. A fifty-five pound bag of this covers about forty square feet to a depth of one inch.[44] Generally chopped bark is a good mulch for perennial beds. Two to three inches is about the right depth when you use most kinds of chopped bark. It needs to be replaced only every couple of years, if you rake it up at the end of the season and save it, instead of tilling it under.

Buckwheat hulls   I have heard several gardeners call this "the ideal mulch." It handles easily, decomposes slowly, and does just about everything a mulch is supposed to do. It is inconspicuous, and can be raked up in the fall and saved for another season. Buckwheat hulls sometimes are sold under the commercial name "Multex," and they are somewhat expensive. A fifty pound bag will cover sixty-five square feet at a one-inch depth. It usually is applied in a layer that is one to three inches thick.

Dick Raymond, my gardening mentor, once remarked to me that using a buckwheat hull mulch just once is like introducing a mild hereditary mental disease into the family. Because the hulls contain an occasional seed or two, rare shoots of buckwheat keep cropping up generations later. But they never seem to amount to much, so this is nothing to worry about.

A buckwheat hull mulch does not retain soil moisture as well as do some other mulches. It also can be blown around a bit in a heavy wind and get splashed about in a real downpour. Because the hulls are dark, they absorb heat and can burn the leaves of succulent young plants that grow close to the ground.

Burlap Burlap is effective for preventing erosion on steep slopes. It is widely used in grass seeding operations, but it is hard to see how it would be of great value in the food-growing garden.

For controlling weeds, it has to be rated somewhere near zero, because grass grows right through it. If you have lots of old burlap feed bags around, you might find use for them as a temporary mulch. But it seems like a waste of money to buy burlap strips. If you plan to grow grass under burlap, leave it there to decompose once the grass has grown.

Cocoa shells Because they are fairly dark in color cocoa shells absorb heat and warm the earth beneath them. They decompose slowly, adding lots of nitrogen, phosphorous, and potassium to the soil as they rot. For a while at least, they give off a chocolate smell. Two to three inches of this mulch is plenty around most plants.

Cocoa shells or hulls retain moisture for long periods of time and get slimy to walk on after about six months in the open. They may pack too, and during periods of high humidity may develop molds on their surface. These are harmless, though unsightly, and can be put out of sight simply by turning the mulch. Another measure for preventing such visible mold is to improve the mulch's texture by mixing two parts shells to one part sawdust or pine needles. Unless you happen to live somewhere near a chocolate-processing factory, you may have to forget it. Cocoa hulls may be too expensive.

Coffee grounds Coffee grounds are a good home-made mulch, even though it may take a while to accumulate enough of them to do you any good. And today, with the popularity of instant coffee, the grounds are not as plentiful as they once were. Used grounds have a very fine consistency and will cake once they are put outside in the weather. Use them lightly—never more than one inch deep—or else air may not be able to reach the plant roots.

Compost Partially-decomposed compost of course is a fantastic "feeding" mulch. After you put it on the garden it will disintegrate quickly and become humus. It adds many nutrients in the process. I have to regard the relative cost of a compost mulch as high. Good compost always is in great demand and the supplies almost always seem to be limited. If your compost-mulch is made up primarily of leaves, it may become matted, if you ignore it for too long without turning it. Then water won't be able to pass through it from above.

Cork, ground Ground cork, as you might expect, is extremely light and easy to handle. It is *so* light in fact, that you might also expect the first breeze would blow it across the countryside and that even a raindrop would dislodge it from place. Surprisingly enough, it stays in place very well once it has been soaked.

Dry or wet, ground cork is completely odorless. Its disintegration is so incredibly slow that it seems like an inert material and its effect on the nitrogen content of the soil hardly can be measured. Like bark, it can be raked up, saved and used from one season to the next. Cork has always been known for its insulating qualities, so it comes as no surprise that ground cork can be classified as excellent in this respect.[45] Unfortunately it is not that easy to find everywhere and might be expensive.

Corncobs, ground; cornstalks, shredded Midwestern gardeners have known for a long time that ground corncobs and stalks make a fine and readily-available mulching material. On the good side: ground cobs are an excellent weed inhibitor and do a good job of retaining soil moisture. On the bad side: its texture makes it somewhat reluctant to let rain water *into* the soil. It's a good idea to wet the soil before you apply this mulch, and add some nitrogen fertilizer while you're at it. Ground corncobs may begin to generate some heat after a while. Keep this mulch away from the stems of tender young things. A three to four-inch layer usually is enough. Don't grind up stalks that have been attacked by borers, disease or worms. Turn them under the soil.

Cottonseed hulls Cottonseed hulls are plentiful and cheap, particularly if you live anywhere near a cotton gin in one of the Southern states. These hulls can be used most effectively around plants, such as beans, which are suited to wide-row planting. (We plant bean and pea seeds four to six abreast in ten to twelve-inch wide rows). After the plants have grown three or four inches high, the mulch can be sifted down through the leaves keeping weeds down in hard-to-reach places. Cottonseed hulls have a fertilizer value which is similar to, though not as rich as, cottonseed meal. Because they are so light the hulls will blow around when there is lots of wind.

Cranberry vines Cranberry vines are sold commercially on Cape Cod, in Wisconsin and in other places where cranberries are grown. The vines can be used whole—they are a little unwieldy this way—or chopped. They are good looking either way. If you use cranberry vines for winter protection, you might want to hold them in place with evergreen boughs. They are wiry and light, they never pack down and they decompose very slowly. This is why they can be used over and over again. Pea vines have similar characteristics.

Evergreen boughs Boughs probably are more attractive as Christmas decorations than as mulch. But they are valuable as winter protection. The Georgia Extension Service recommends them for erosion prevention, too. If you do use boughs to anchor the winter snow on your perennials, you probably will want to replace them with something else in the spring. They will have turned brown and ugly by then anyway.

Fiberglass Fiberglass is completely fireproof. It also is quite costly and nonbiodegradeable. It is pretty hard for me to imagine anything less attractive than strips of pink, aluminum-faced fiberglass building insulation lying in a lush green garden. If you ever have handled the stuff, particularly on a hot day, you can understand why carpenters always like to have their apprentices do the insulating in a new house. The itchiness from the fiberglass is enough to drive you up the nearest wall.

When it is wet, fiberglass insulation absorbs water like a sponge and then compacts. The only thing to recommend it, really, is its superior insulating quality. There are some commercially-made fiberglass mats for sale which are designed specifically to be used as mulch. Some of them have holes for plants (and weeds) to grow through. Some do not.

Grass clippings Almost anyone with a yard has grass clippings. Next to peat moss and hay, this probably is the most frequently-mentioned kind of mulch. Spring clippings can be used as a thinly-spread mulch as your first vegetable seedlings come up. They will provide good nutrients and the fine grass will not choke the tiny plants the way a thicker, coarser mulch might. It is better to dry grass clippings first. If they are spread too thickly they will make a hot slimy mess.[46] Not only that, they will smell bad.

Otherwise grass clippings are a good, cheap mulch, and they are already chopped for you if you use a rotary lawn mower. Some gardeners like to mix them with peat moss to slow down what would otherwise be a very rapid rate of decomposition.

Green ground covers Appearance: excellent. Insulation value: only fair. These low-growing plants include things like thyme, violets, pachysandra, sweet woodruff, myrtle, and Johnny-jump-ups. Pachysandra is pretty expensive and spreads very slowly, but the cost of myrtle is not so high. One associate of ours complains, though, that myrtle spreads its lateral roots so fast that it sometimes takes over adjacent vegetables.

A few weeds will grow among these live green ground covers until the plants become firmly entrenched. Then they grow so thick that nothing else has a chance. Once you have a patch of something like pachysandra growing well, removing six or eight plants to start a new patch somewhere else is like taking a bucket of water out of a well. You will never notice they are gone. Try these. They are not a bad mulch, if you use them in places where you are not going to be doing a lot of walking.

Growing green mulches At Garden Way we often call these "green manures," meaning cover crops. The price of this seed is low, so we plant cover crops for winter protection in some parts of our garden plots. In the fall we till in leaves along with whatever summer mulch is left in the garden, and we plant buckwheat, annual rye grass or winter rye. In the spring the perennials can be cut, dried, chopped and used later as mulch. Sometimes we leave the stubble in place until just be-

GREEN MANURES. In the spring they can be harvested, dried, chopped and used later as mulch.

fore we get ready to plant. Sometimes we till the whole cover crop directly into the soil where it decomposes quickly. Later we mulch with other materials.

Hay Hay probably has been used longer than any other mulching material. And undoubtedly it always has looked as unsightly as it does today. Chopped hay looks much better.

First cut hay—First cut hay normally has been allowed to go to seed. Many gardeners are reluctant to use it as mulch because it introduces a horde of weed and grass seeds into the garden. Ruth Stout, as you'll remember, argues long and hard that if the mulch is kept thick enough—as much as eight to ten inches—very few weeds will find their way through, regardless of the number of seeds in the mulch. Usually you don't have to *add* more hay. Lift what is already there, fluff it, and put it back down on top of the weeds.

Second or third cut hay—Second or third cut hay often is harvested before it has had a chance to go to seed. If you can get it, you might feel a little better about using this on your garden. All hay decomposes fairly rapidly and boosts the nitrogen content of the soil—although if it is quite fresh it will rob nitrogen for a short period of time when it is just starting to rot. Partially-rotted hay makes better mulch than fresh hay for just this reason. Leave some fresh bales outside through the winter. In the spring they will be weathered and damp. Seedless hay is desirable for mulching raspberries, grapes, and young fruit trees. Make friends with a local farmer. He may be glad to get rid of any hay that has spoiled and is unfit to feed to his livestock. Have you noticed how much cut hay (some of it is weeds) there is along the sides of roads in late summer? Rake it up! It's free for the taking.

Hops, spent Spent hops, which is nothing but a waste product as far as a brewery is concerned, is an inexpensive mulch wherever it is available. It decays very slowly and needs to be renewed only every three or four years if you apply it four to six inches thick, and later rake it up and save it. You also might find that it has an objectionable odor at first. It is very resistant to fire because it tends to stay damp, and this makes it an ideal mulch for conserving soil moisture. Spent hops can generate an overdose of heat to your very small plants, so keep it a little way away from them.

There is one odd drawback to spent hops, and if you live in an urban area you might want to think twice about using it. It is very hard to keep in place because pigeons—believe it or not—find some food material in hops which is to their liking. They will pick it over continually and spread it all over your yard and lawn. This was such a problem in the Boston Botanical Gardens that they were forced to quit using it as a mulch.[47]

Leaves It seems almost criminal to burn leaves. They are nature's favorite mulching material. They contain many of the essential trace mineral elements which the long, penetrating tree roots have retrieved from the deep subsoil. In addition to the basic nutrients that all plants need—nitrogen, phosphorous, and potassium—leaves also have such minerals as boron, cobalt and magnesium in much smaller amounts.

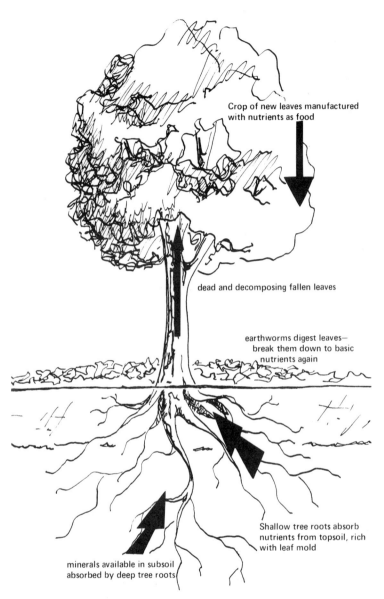

Crop of new leaves manufactured with nutrients as food

dead and decomposing fallen leaves

earthworms digest leaves— break them down to basic nutrients again

Shallow tree roots absorb nutrients from topsoil, rich with leaf mold

minerals available in subsoil absorbed by deep tree roots

THE LIFE CYCLE OF A LEAF. Leaves, in any state of decomposition, make excellent mulch. They contain many of the essential trace mineral elements which the long penetrating tree roots have retrieved from the subsoil. In addition to the basic nutrients that all plants need—nitrogen, phosphorous and potassium—leaves also have such minerals as boron, cobalt and magnesium.

Maple, birch and elm leaves tend to mat and become soggy. If these are chopped, the water and air can penetrate them more easily, and the danger of developing crown rot in some plants is lessened. Oak, beech and sycamore leaves don't mat so badly, but they too are more satisfactory if chopped. There is no law which forbids mixing leaves with straw, ground corn cobs, pine needles or some other light material to improve the consistency of the mulch.[48] Leaves in any state of decomposition make a splendid mulch.

Leaf mold What is the difference between leaves and leaf mold? Leaf mold has disintegrated to the point where the leaves are no longer distinguishable, and just the skeletal system of the leaf is left. Leaf mold is sometimes available from municipalities which stockpile the leaves that have been gathered from along streets and in parks. Be a little careful with them. They may contain lead from automobile exhaust, and this is toxic. Leaves that have been rotting for a long time in a pile which has been rarely if ever turned, tend to be very matted and not well-decomposed.

Rich leaf mold can be put to good use in feeding perennial plants that are difficult or impossible to cultivate, like grapes, berries, and fruit trees. Leaf mold which has been mixed into the soil before seed planting can produce a spectacular effect on the growth of some plants.

Manure Most of us think of manure more as a fertilizer than as a mulch. It does supply all *kinds* of plant food, but it can fulfill many of the requirements of a good mulch too. Most animal manures are mixed with straw, sawdust or some other absorptive material which has been used as bedding. Unfortunately manure is in great demand, and what used to be free for the trucking, now is sometimes hard to find.

The best manure is well-rotted. Don't forget: If you use good, well-rotted manure as mulch, it will encourage the growth of weeds in the same way that it encourages the growth of any plant. Manure that has had no time to age can burn plants and will smell awful. Be a little careful with the dried, packaged varieties, too. They have been known to contain harmful salts.

Muck Muck is black organic matter that has been retrieved from swampy areas. Its characteristics are similar to "sludge"—another highly-fertile material—which is the product of sewage treatment plants. Muck sometimes is packaged in polyethylene bags and sold commercially. Once it dries it becomes a fine dust which can blow around or be washed away by rain. Muck also disintegrates fast and needs to be renewed often. Both of these negative qualities can be improved if you mix muck with something else to give it more density.

Oak leaf mulch Some organic gardeners make a point of keeping their oak leaves separate from others, to use them as a pest-controlling mulch. John and Helen Philbrick write that an oak leaf mulch "produces an atmosphere which slugs and cut worms and June bug grubs and other very tender ones just cannot stand. Perhaps these tender-bodied creatures just feel puckery all over when surrounded by bitter leaves like oak."[49]

Oyster shells, ground A lady named Ruth Bixler had trouble keeping anything growing in the shale soil of her Pennsylvania home. She says,

"One Saturday I stopped at the feed store to get some food for our rabbit, and right in front of me I saw the answer— bags of ground oyster shells. I bought bag after bag and started shaking it over my soil. I really put it on thick and it was beautiful for the summer; not even a heavy shower disturbed it. . . . The roses were never more beautiful and bloomed until the first snow . . . My Mimosa trees got through the severe winter without a single loss." . . .[50]

Exactly what aphrodisiac affect the oyster shells had on her Mimosas, she does not say. Her success with them might be explained by the fact that oyster shells are "basic" or "alkaline." This means they have a high pH and operate like lime to neutralize acid soils. But there seems to be no reason why this mulch would not work well on vegetables, especially in soils with a low pH.

Paper   Paper which is produced especially to be used as mulch first was developed for pineapple plantations in Hawaii. It is treated to make it waterproof and is particularly valuable as a weed controller. But I'm sorry to say that special farm equipment is needed to lay it neatly and efficiently over large areas.

Biodegradable black paper—This is a product which we have tried. It comes in different widths and has a line of neat round holes cut down the center of the roll.

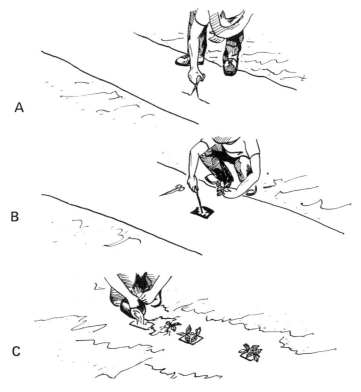

COMMERCIAL MULCH PAPER IN THE HOME GARDEN.
Lay the paper by hand and cut holes (A). Prepare the soil beneath the holes with some small tool (B). Add fertilizer mixed with water and make the transplant (C). Be sure that all the edges of the paper are well covered with soil.

A   B

THE GARBAMAT. This giant disposer (A) transformed trash and water into a fertile mulch which would be used as a side dressing (B).

These, naturally, are to accommodate plants. It seems to work in much the same way as black polyethylene and is certainly no more difficult to hold in place than plastic. It stays intact throughout the growing season. But then does *not* decompose on its own as readily as the manufacturer indicates it's supposed to. Once over lightly with a roto-tiller though, and it pulverizes. It is not advertized as having any particular fertilizer value, and we have done no analysis to see exactly *what* it contains.

Newspaper, etc.—The home gardener can use shredded paper as mulch. Newspaper, for example, is an organic material as are most paper products, and even the ink provides trace elements which are essential to healthy plant life. Mulching with waste paper offers a great opportunity to recycle those stacks of newspaper that might be gathering dust in your basement. True, paper that is shredded by machine is not particularly attractive, but it looks better than newspaper laid in folded sheets between rows of plants. It is also more pervious to water. Paper mulch always can be covered with a little soil to hide it and keep it from blowing. One lady we know uses newspaper to cover her entire garden, covers it with hay and then pokes holes through it with a ski pole to plant seeds. When everything is picked in the fall, she simply tills the whole works under.

Paper pulp Waste paper, sawdust and other trash can be converted into a "mobile, flowing slurry" by combining it with water and grinding it up. Years ago someone developed a machine called the "Garbamat," which was like a gigantic garbage disposer for just this purpose. The invention never was widely distributed, but the stuff it produced was found to be a very fertile mulch, and was used as a side dressing.

F.W. Shumacher of Sandwich, Massachusetts uses wastepaper products from the home and kitchen in deep holes he digs for trees and shrubs. He adds a layer of paper pulp, then a layer of soil, until the bottom portion of the hole is filled. The paper disintegrates adding humus to the soil.[51]

Peanut hulls Peanut hulls are available throughout much of the Southern United States. Alone they make an attractive coarse-looking mulch. Sometimes they are mixed with sawdust or pine needles. They weather quickly, decompose rapidly and add good rich humus to the soil. They contain considerable amounts of nitrogen, phosphorous and potassium. According to some studies, they make a very good mulch for tomato plants.[52] There does not seem to be much to prevent our recommending peanut hulls as a mulch. Use them if they are available where you live. One possible drawback is that they might be attractive to rodents if not completely free of peanuts.

Peat moss Mention the word "mulch" to someone, and he is likely to reply automatically, "Oh yes, you mean peat moss." It's too bad that peat moss and mulching are synonymous in so many peoples' minds. Actually peat moss has very few qualities to recommend it as a surface mulch—although there are lots of things to recommend it as a *soil conditioner*. Clean and easy to handle, it is a valuable aid in deep-planting operations when it is mixed with surface soil and

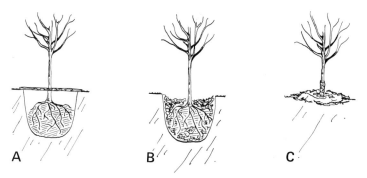

Use peat moss as a soil conditioner when you plant fruit trees. Set the tree in the ground at the same depth it was before transplanting. Use a stick for a depth guide if you need to (A). Fill the hole with a soupy mixture of new topsoil, peat moss and water (B). Mulch immediately and protect the trunk against pests.

water. Trees and shrubs should do very well when they are planted in just this sort of soupy mixture. You should not have to prune the roots at all.

Peat moss is extremely slow to decompose. It is slightly acidic, but it does *not* sour your soil unless used continuously and in great quantities. It has practically zero value as an organic fertilizer, adding little or no nutrients to the soil. A ninety-five pound bale of pressed peat spread one inch thick will cover about three hundred square feet. Soil under it should be thoroughly moist before peat moss is applied. Once it *is* in place it should be kept moist and loose or it may dry out and form an impervious crust. When it is loose, peat moss is astonishingly absorptive. It can soak up six to twelve *times* its weight in water! In other words, it takes an awfully heavy rainstorm to provide enough water to percolate through a peat moss mulch. To be blunt: Find something better—and cheaper—to mulch with.

Pine needles Pine needles should be available for the raking. They are light, clean, weed-free and easy to handle. *White pine* trees have soft flexible needles that make fine mulch. Needles from the *red pine* are coarser

and may not rot for several years, but are good for mulching larger plants. *Cedar* trees drop fine but wider "leaves" which make a great mulch for windy places. If you have ever tried sweeping them off a roof or walkway you know all about their affinity for staying put.

Pine needles absorb little or no moisture themselves, so water trickles through them easily. They can be used more than once because they decompose so slowly. Unfortunately there seems to be very little worm activity under a pine needle mulch. Pine needles traditionally have been used around acid loving plants, but—just to repeat what has been said so many times already—they do not lower the soil pH so much that you should hesitate to use them on other plants as well.

Polyethylene Polyethylene can be transparent, "aluminized," dark green or black. Black plastic seems to be used more often than anything else. Because no light penetrates its opaque surface, *no* weeds can grow beneath it the way they might under clear plastic.

Studies done in our sister state at the University of New Hampshire show that its dark color absorbs the heat of the sun, causing the soil temperature to rise anywhere from three to seven degrees F. on a sunny day.[53] Authorities here at the University of Vermont, on the other hand, have argued on several occasions that the heat is given off to the atmosphere above the plastic because a layer of air—which inevitably winds up under the plastic unless you take special precautions to keep it out—acts as insulation. In either case, plastic of any color practically eliminates moisture evaporation. Water condenses on the under side and drips back into the soil. This also tends to keep the seedbed in a friable condition.

Most folks who use it, lay the plastic before they plant, being sure the soil is fairly moist first. Be certain,

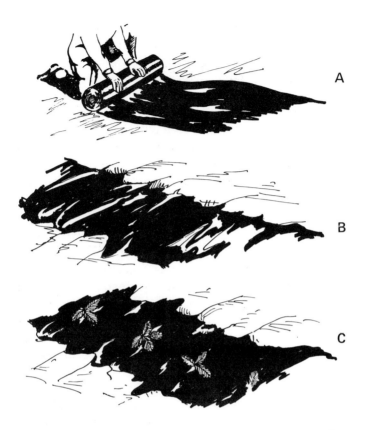

*BLACK POLYETHYLENE MULCH. Lay the plastic before you plant,
being sure the soil is fairly moist first (A). Be certain that it is weighted
down properly and that all edges are covered with dirt so the wind can't get
under it and blow it away (B). Cut round, X-shaped or T-shaped holes in
the film so plants can grow up and water can go down.*

if you try plastic mulching, that it is weighted down
properly and that all the edges are covered with dirt so
the wind can't get under it and blow it away. Cut
round, X-shaped or T-shaped holes in the plastic film
so plants can grow up and water can go down.

No polyethylene will decompose at all. So it can have
no positive *or* negative chemical effects on the soil.
After the growing season—I'm sorry to say—you will
be confronted with the unpleasant task of pulling up
wet, dirty plastic and storing it for the winter.

Poultry litter A local organic gardener of considerable renown, by the name of Jim Price, uses poultry litter with great success, though he chooses to refer to it by a different name, which courtesy does not allow me to mention here. But it is all the same stuff no matter what you call it. Frankly I was amazed at the size of his cabbages and onions grown with it.

Poultry litter might consist of straw, sawdust, shavings, crushed corncobs plus the manure itself, but primarily it is the manure in this concoction that supplies nitrogen to the soil. The fact that it *is* a mixture is important. Straight manure might damage plants by giving them an *overdose* of fertilizer. Poultry litter still is available at very low cost from many poultry farms.

Pyrophyllite Pyrophyllite is calcine clay particles which can be purchased in a fine-grained sand or in 1 to 1½-inch chunks. If you see bags of "Terra-Green Jumbos—Decorative Surface Mulch" in your local hardware or feed store, it is pyrophyllite. The pitch on the bag reads, ". . . Composed of 100% pure, inorganic, inert, non-flammable prophyllite absorbent. Controlled high temperature processing insures stability and sterility." Calcine clay should be considered a more-or-less permanent mulch, and it is about as "decorative" as adobe. If you really *like* adobe, consider buying some. Otherwise buy gravel. It's cheaper and won't absorb so much water.

Redwood bark, chips Redwood is most abundant on the West coast, but now redwood and redwood by-products can be found anywhere in the country. It is fairly expensive when sold in packages. You can buy it in several forms: as ground bark, as chips or as "nuggets." Redwood is a most attractive mulch in any of its various textures. It is not a particularly good source of humus, because it is extremely rot-resistant.

Some people have complained that water runs off redwood chips just as off the back of the proverbial duck, and that not enough water gets to the soil. Earthworms avoid redwood in much the same way that they avoid the leaves from coniferous trees. If you have an insect problem in your garden and don't like the idea of inorganic insecticides, using redwood mulch may be one approach to your problem. In some cases it acts as a bug repellent.

Incidentally: Douglas fir bark has many characteristics which make it similar to redwood bark. It is sold in plastic bags under the trade name "Silvamulch."

Salt hay   Salt hay or salt straw is light, clean, pest-free and longlasting. It too can be used a second or third time. It never seems to get matted or soggy, and water penetrates it easily. It makes an exceptionally good winter mulch. A bale of salt hay will provide a light covering for an area of about twelve-hundred square feet. A three to six-inch covering should be more than enough.

Salt marsh hay is expensive if you buy it, but free if you cut it or gather it yourself. It floats on the marshes and is left along the edges by high winds and high tides. If you live along a marshy coast, you probably can go out and collect truckloads of it after a storm.

Sawdust   Dick Raymond refuses even to consider using sawdust as a mulch in the vegetable garden, mostly because, as he claims, it is so unattractive to worms. Sawdust also has other disadvantages. It takes quite a long time to decompose unless it is tilled into the soil. It might encourage crown rot in some plants because it can hold moisture against the stem. It often is splashed up onto plants by raindrops, too. It is a fire hazard if used too thickly—say in layers of more than three inches. Water penetration through sawdust is only fair. In fact, some have complained that a sawdust mulch actually will draw moisture back *up* out of the soil. Sawdust does have a high carbon content, but is *not* toxic.

If you have a ready supply of sawdust that you were planning to use as mulch, don't be completely discouraged. There are ways of getting around some of these problems. Sawdust is not such a bad mulch if it is "inoculated" with calcium nitrate or sodium nitrate. Sawdust that splashes on plants usually falls back off as soon as it dries. *Unweathered* pine sawdust does decompose very slowly. So just give it some time to weather and turn gray before you use it. Hardwood sawdust, by the way, rots much more rapidly than pine or spruce or cedar, especially if it is weathered. "Cut" sawdust with other mulching materials, if you like. To reassure you further, studies have shown that the tannins and terpenes in sawdust which gardeners have feared for years, actually harm the soil very little. Any sawdust or shavings that have been used for cattle bedding make super mulch.[54]

Seaweed, kelp There doesn't seem to be any way that seaweed can improve the cosmetics of your garden unless it is finely chopped. It *is* an excellent winter mulch and a great material for sheet composting. In most coastal areas it is free.

If the kelp you gather on the beach is *loaded* with salt, you might do well to rinse it off once or twice with your garden hose. But don't worry about getting it entirely salt-free. What salt is left probably will benefit rather than harm your soil. Seaweed donates potash, among other things, as it disintegrates. It also provides sodium, boron, iodine and other trace elements.

Stinging nettle mulch The Philbricks write,

Home gardeners who find the stinging nettle will not grow for them may still enjoy some of its benefits by importing stinging nettle from another garden to mulch certain plants. It is even practical to bring "nettle soil" from the wood to scatter around plants in the backyard garden. The extra vitality which the nettle imparts to all its surrounding plants is remarkable and instead of trying to get rid of it, we should all learn to appreciate it and use it for its helpful [insect-repelling] qualities.[55]

Stone Stone includes gravel, shale, crushed marble or limestone, even rocks and flagstones. It can be one of the most decorative mulches. It is no longer cheap in most cases, but you can buy it in all sorts of textures and colors. As we have all seen, weeds find their way through crushed stone pretty easily—although shale is an exception.

Stone retains heat from the sun. It will warm the soil under it well into a cool evening. Stone obviously should be considered a permanent mulch. A few trace elements might leach out of a stone mulch over a period of years, but unless you use limestone, it probably is not going to dissolve noticeably in your lifetime. Use it where you are sure you will not till, such as around ornamental shrubbery and fruit trees.

"Conkilite" is a trade name for lime or marble pebbles that come in small, medium, or large stones. As advertised, this gives a "formalized" appearance when it is used as a mulch, but they recommend using eight pounds per square *foot!*

Straw Ideally, straw should be seed-free and chopped. A layer of chopped straw needs to be only about an inch and a half thick. Loose straw can be as much as six to eight inches thick, but is tough to handle and does not give a very tidy appearance. In either case, unless the straw is very weathered, add some high-nitrogen fertilizer to the soil first.

Two things you should not forget about straw mulch: (1) It can be a fire hazard, and (2) Because of its high seed content, oat straw mulches usually are pretty ineffectual as weed controllers—unless of course, you are *trying* to grow more oats.

Sugar cane Sugar cane residue, often called "bagasse," consists of cane stalks that have been pressed, heated, and ground. Sometimes it is packaged and sold under the name "Servall", and the cost is moderate. Sugar cane somehow never seems to weather or darken, but retains its very light color, which some people find objectionable. It has a pH which is somewhere between 4.5 and 5.2, so it would not do a bit of harm to add a little lime to your soil if your plans include extensive use of a bagasse mulch. Like peat moss, it is highly absorbent and will hold about three-and-a-half times its weight in water. Other than that, it makes a pretty satisfactory mulch. It will rot quickly because of the sugar content, so it needs frequent replenishment.

Tobacco stems The nicotine in tobacco leaves is equally present in tobacco stems which you can buy from some seed companies. The stems are coarse and easy to handle, and their presence in a mulch will repel aphids, flea bettles, thrips and other insects.[56] Tobacco stems are widely used, needless to say, in areas where tobacco is grown. They can be left on the garden over the winter, if you like, where rains and snows will leach nutrients from the stalks into the ground.[57] What is left of them can be raked up in the spring and used again. Tobacco stems also can be ground. Use only half an inch of ground stems, two to three inches otherwise. Tobacco stems decompose quite readily, stealing a little nitrogen at first.

Vermiculite Vermiculite (or "perlite" which is similar) can be a very good mulch, which we heartily recommend for hothouse use. Outdoors it is not so good. It is so light that it splashes around in a rainstorm. Nonetheless some gardeners claim they have used it very successfully in very dry, very hot places outside. A layer of half an inch to an inch is enough. Vermiculite is fairly costly and almost totally sterile, which means that it will contribute virtually nothing to the soil in the way of fertilizer.

Walnut shells Ground or whole walnut shells last a long time. Pecan and almond shells are very much the same. All are cinnamon brown in color and make a pleasing appearance. They don't wash away, they are fire resistant, and they are rot resistant. They absorb very little moisture themselves, so water percolation into the soil is good. One or two inches of walnut shells is plenty. Walnut and pecan shell mulches also might furnish some good minerals during their super-slow rotting process. Use them for several years.

Wood chips   Wood chips from a brush chipper generally make excellent mulch. Regrettably they are not a cheap item anymore. It used to be that cities and towns, which even would compost the chips, would let you have them for nothing if you were willing to haul them away. At the New York Botanical Gardens in the Bronx wood chip mulch is stolen from beneath plants faster than the gardeners can put it there. They suspect little old ladies with spoons and buckets.

Wood chips naturally decompose more slowly than sawdust and, therefore, deplete the nitrogen content in the soil very little. To repeat what was said earlier: Yes, there *can* be carpenter ants and similar creatures in wood chips. No, wood chips do not retain tree diseases, not even Dutch elm disease.

Wood shavings   Wood shavings can be the thinly-curled stuff you sweep off the floor next to a cabinet maker's bench or the coarse material from a woodshop jointer or planing machine. It might also be the fluffy shredded wooden packing material sometimes called "excelsior."

Hardwood shavings are superior to the softwood shavings from pine, cedar or spruce, which are notoriously-voracious nitrogen thieves: The thinest shavings are the worst offenders. They are somewhat less gluttonous if you mix them with cottonseed meal, alfalfa meal or a chemical fertilizer. We recommend chips over shavings if you like the idea of using a wood-base mulch.

Our friend Ted Flanagan,[58] agronomist and vegetable expert at the University of Vermont in Burlington, tells me that his father is probably the best mulching material scrounger in all the world. "My father will mulch with *anything!*" he says. But I can't help wondering if the elder Flanagan isn't second to his son in mulching inventiveness.

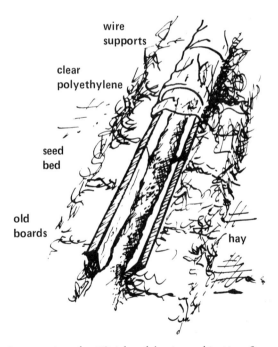

Try using organic and artificial mulches in combination. Some plants can be started outdoors well before the last killing frost by using this "poorman's cold frame". The boards catch the heat of the spring sun, the hay acts as insulation, and the plastic protects the seedlings from frost.

Ted has a marvelous collection of mulches which are neatly displayed in shoe boxes with impressive engraved plastic labels on them. Actually it is a very valuable display in spite of the grief we give him about it, and he was kind enough to let me photograph the entire collection.

The collection includes rotting boards, old cedar shingles, paper bags—complete with printed advertisements for stores in downtown Burlington, wrapping paper (from the same stores, no doubt), paper towels, paper napkins, magazines, underlayment paper, corrogated cardboard (in rolls as well as in strips), shirt cardboards, stump chippings (which he distinguishes somehow from other wood chips), kitty litter, algae (from Lake Champlain I think), dried silage (which seems to have distinct disadvantages), and a license plate (1968 Vermont registration #1045). Can you think of anything he's left out? What would a psychologist say of a garden mulched with Flanagan pop-art?

[7]

how annual vegetables can be mulched

Here is a list of annual vegetables that we in Charlotte are reasonably familiar with. Each item on the list is followed by a discussion of how and when these vegetables *might* be mulched.⁵⁹

While considering each of the suggestions made here, keep several things in mind: (1) The general mulching guidelines offered in the earlier chapters, (2) Your *own* experience with a particular vegetable, (3) The climate in your part of the country, and (4) The idiosyncracies of your garden, such as the soil condition, drainage, the amount of sunlight and the likelihood of certain pests. As always, I will try to resist telling you what to do, and will leave you the burden of deciding *if* and *how* and *when* to mulch *what* in your garden.

Just so this doesn't sound like a *total* cop-out, let me say I think you will find lots of useful information here that you can adapt to your own situation.

Asparagus   See the chapter on perennial plants.

Beans   Dick Raymond says, "Beans generally take care of themselves." He seems to be right, but if you pin him down, he will admit that they should be mulched in a dry year with something like chopped straw. This can be done about two or three weeks after planting.

Mulching is beneficial to beans especially because it inhibits weed growth. The finer the mulch the better, if you like to plant beans in wide rows the way we often do. Bean roots grow close to the surface, and any deep or extensive cultivation to halt weeds will result in undesirable root pruning of the beans themselves.

Arthur Burrage, the famous New England gardener and writer from Ipswich, Massachusetts, says,

> We found that the use of a thick mulch of about four inches of salt marsh straw or salt marsh hay is well worthwhile. It improves the quality, increases the yield, and completely eliminates the need for weeding—once the mulch is laid down.

In Charlotte we have had trouble growing lima beans. We seem to get a germination which is no better than about forty percent, and the yield is low, too. If you have luck with them where you are, your lima beans can be mulched with about three inches of a light organic material as soon as they are four inches high.

We do plant lots of soybeans here—in wide rows or just broadcast. Left to their own devices, as Dick says, they do just fine. So we don't bother to mulch them, though I'm sure mulch would do no harm. Same with pole beans.

After planting some rows of beans in clear ground in my own garden this year, I poke-planted a wide row of green snap beans with my finger, through a walkway of hay books. I was a man of little faith, so the next day I went back to pull the books apart and loosen the hay a bit. The beans came up through the mulch just as quickly and apparently just as easily as those that had no mulch. Since then they have grown every bit as strong, if not stronger than their unmulched counterparts. In fact, in spite of this extraordinarily wet season, they look greener and healthier. Possibly it is because fewer nutrients were leached out of the soil under the mulch by the torrents of rain we had. I should have been more of a believer, for had I left the books of hay more intact, I'll bet I would have fewer weeds among those beans now.

Beets Beets like alkaline soil. So probably it is better not to mulch them with pine needles, oak and beech leaves, or peat moss exclusively. Use just about anything else. In fact, adding ground limestone or lime to the soil or mixing it with the mulch may be a good idea. Arthur Burrage says that "the use of mulch on the beet bed pays greater dividends than anywhere else on the garden." Ideally leaves or leaf compost should be spread on beet plots at least once a year and worked into the soil as fertilizer.

A light mulch of grass clippings can be put down right after planting beet seeds, to conserve moisture and prevent the sun from baking the soil hard. As soon as the sprouts appear, pull this mulch back a bit for a while, because beets are very susceptible to damping off. As the growing season progresses, increase the thickness of the mulch by adding more layers of straw or hay, and some time after the rows have been thinned, tuck it in close to the maturing plants. This procedure seems to work well for turnips and rutabagas, too.

Beets do poorly in soil that is deficient in boron. A seaweed mulch can correct this shortage in a few weeks.

Beets respond badly to boron shortages in the soil. Chopped kelp (seaweed) is an excellent organic mulch which can correct this deficiency in a few weeks. Beets also thrive in humus-rich soil, and continuous mulching, of course, will contribute to this condition in your soil.

Blueberries   See the chapter on perennial plants.

Broccoli   Broccoli can be mulched shortly after the plants have been moved out of the cold frame or greenhouse and set out in the garden. Any non-acid organic mulch is fine. It will preserve moisture and discourage some insects. Late in the season, because broccoli is naturally frost-resistant, the mulch can extend a plant's productive time. Broccoli can stand a maximum of four to six inches of organic mulch.

Polyethylene works well with broccoli. If you use it, lay the plastic, cut holes, and transplant through the openings. A little fertilizer and lime beforehand probably is in order.

Cabbage   After your transplants are well established, partially-decomposed mulch can be tucked right up under the leaves around your cabbage plants. This may slow their growth somewhat, but they will grow tender, green and succulent.

According to the Agricultural Experimental Station at the University of Connecticut, an aluminum foil mulch is especially suitable for cabbage. It discourages some disease-carrying aphids.

Cabbage—which is somewhat frost-resistant—can be stored upright in a shallow trench that is framed with stakes and boards. Pull the plants out of the garden by the roots, and set them side by side in the trench. Pack soil around the roots. Next bank soil around the frame, and finally, place boards across the top of the frame to hold a covering of straw, hay, or leaves.

If you live in a warm climate location—one that normally experiences mild winters—you might like to plant cabbage seed and cover the beds with a mulch sometime in the late fall—in November or early December. Re-cover the bed with coarser mulch, such as twigs or evergreen boughs, as soon as the seedlings appear. In spring, when you uncover them, you will have some hardy babies for early transplanting.[60]

Cantaloupes Everyone seems to agree that cantaloupes and other melons need lots of moisture as well as heat—from the time they come up until they are fully grown. Advocates of plastic mulch feel they get an earlier and larger yield by using their black polyethylene film. This, they say, is especially helpful when the spring is cool and dry. The film helps to warm the soil, eliminates weeds and maintains a more constant supply of water to the roots.

A thick organic mulch is designed to do pretty much the same thing. Hay, grass clippings, buckwheat hulls, cocoa shells and newspapers work fine. It probably is better to stay away from sawdust and leaves. The mulch should be in place before the fruit develops, since handling may damage the tender melons. Once the fruit is formed, it will be resting on a clean carpet of mulch and won't be as prone to rot.

Dick Raymond likes to see melon plants maintain contact with the soil because he feels the runners themselves absorb moisture and nourishment from the ground. So he discourages the use of plastic or any organic mulch that the runners can not be tucked under easily. In fact, in a normal year, he would prefer no mulch at all at least until the fruit has started to form. Then to keep the fruit clean, he would very carefully set the melon on top of a tin can. This, he tells me, makes them sweeter. He doesn't know why exactly, but thinks it might have something to do with the melons getting more uniform heat. A tin can mulch, you say? How could Ted Flanagan have missed that one?

Carrots Mulch should be used very sparingly on carrots. When you sow them, you might want to spread a very thin mulch, say of grass clippings, over the beds to prevent the soil surface from forming a crust that the sprouting seeds can't break through. Water this mulch if you like, but be careful that the tiny seeds don't wash away. When the slender seedlings come up, be sure that the mulch does not interfere with them.

The Rodale Press offers an interesting suggestion for mulching carrots:

> If you are tired of the pesky brown worm that spoils your carrots, you might be able to foil it with a coffee break. Mix your package of carrot seed with one cup of fresh, unused coffee grounds. Plant the coffee with your seeds. It won't flavor the carrots as sprays and other poisonous substances do. Because coffee grounds are acid, they are good for plants that like that kind of treatment. Often it is best to mix ground limestone with the grounds before using it as a mulch or top dressing.

Have you tried leaving your carrots in the ground during the early winter months to save storage space in the house? They can be kept there, covered with a heavy mulch of some kind. Many people prefer them to the frozen or canned stuff you get at the supermarket.

Cauliflower Cauliflower can be mulched in much the same way as broccoli. Mulch right to the lower leaves shortly after transplanting or lay plastic and plant through it.

Cauliflower can stand four to six inches of organic mulch. Because it is naturally frost-resistant, a heavy mulch on cauliflower can extend the plant's productive time.

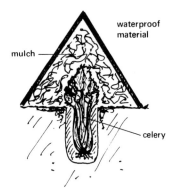

waterproof material

mulch

celery

In the fall store celery beneath a deep mulch which is protected by some waterproof material. This way you can dig celery as you want it—even in midwinter.

Celery   The traditional way to "blanch" celery is with a dust mulch. Earth is pulled around the plants as they get higher, until finally, when the celery is full grown, the celery rows are about eighteen inches high and only the green tops are showing. As a cleaner alternative, try an organic mulch rather than dirt to blanch your celery. Chopped leaves, which are less translucent than something like hay, are best. Whole leaves may dry out and blow away.

Celery that is protected with a deep mulch will produce crisp tender hearts until Thanksgiving time or later. Ideally the heavily-mulched rows should be covered with sheet metal, plastic or some other waterproof material, to form something like a tent. By protecting the ground this way, it stays dry and will not freeze too hard. There is no problem digging celery any time you want it, even in mid-winter. You shovel away some snow, remove the tent, and uncover as much celery as you want to eat. Celery that is protected this way keeps better than in a root cellar.

Chard   (See spinach.)

Corn   Some gardeners like Ruth Stout favor keeping a permanent organic mulch on their corn patches. At planting time they just run a straight line with a string, and push their corn seeds down through the mulch with the index finger. After the harvest, Mrs. Stout at least, simply breaks the stalks over with her foot and throws more hay over the old mulch.

Permanent mulchers argue that crows seem to be nonplussed by the heavy layer of mulch over corn. They normally will pull small corn plants nearly as fast as they show above ground. If the corn has had a chance to get a good headstart under mulch, the plants, will yield disappointing results to the average crow who is after those tender sprouted kernels below the plants.

Here in Charlotte, where we worry about soil warmth until as late as early June, we plant corn in the bottom of a furrow and use no mulch for a while. We cover the seed with about an inch of soil—which doesn't begin to fill the furrow—and stretch twelve-inch chicken wire over the top of the furrow. The birds are unable or unwilling to reach the planted kernels or shoots through the wire. If you have no way to make a furrow (we just use the little furrower that attaches to the back of a roto-tiller), buy some twenty-four-inch chicken wire, and bend it down the middle to make an inverted "V" and form a tent over your row of corn. Be sure to close off the ends, or the birds will get in there and saunter nonchalantly down each row picking kernels of corn seed out of the ground as they go.

According to the old maxim, corn should be "knee high by the Fourth of July." At just about this point—when the corn is "tall enough to shade the ground", as Dick says—the corn is mulched. The stalks have been spaced or thinned carefully so they can be mulched without damage. The wire, of course, long-since has been taken up. Use any mulch that will preserve moisture, and give the corn an extra boost by adding nutrients to the soil.

Cucumbers Chopped leaves, leaf mold, straw and old hay are good for mulching cucumbers. Mulch somehow seems to keep cucumber beetles away. It can be put around the plants when they are about three inches high and before the vines really start to extend. Cucumbers, of course, require much moisture, which the mulch will help to retain. Some organic mulches, as you already know, will invite some slugs, snails, diseases, and insects other than the cucumber beetle to your "cukes". To be on the safe side with them, keep the mulch three or four inches away from the main plant.

Eggplant is very finicky. If there is too little moisture around its roots, the leaves turn yellow, become spotted and drop off. If there is too much the plant will not bear fruit. Mulch can help regulate the moisture supply.

Eggplant   Eggplant, especially if it is grown in the North, needs all the warmth it can get. Don't mulch it until after the ground really has had a chance to warm up. Also, the earth immediately around eggplant cannot be disturbed if it is to develop properly. Once the soil is warm enough, mulch will smother most weeds before they grow big enough to be pulled (which would disturb the eggplant roots, too). These finicky plants have roots which prefer to grow and feed in the top two inches of soil. If there is too little moisture there, the leaves turn yellow, become spotted and drop off. If it has too much, it will not bear fruit. Mulch can help to keep a uniform supply of moisture there. Eggplant is also apt to attract flea beetles. Aluminum, laid temporarily on top of other mulch, has been known to foil these insects.

Fruit trees   See the chapter on perennial plants.

Garlic   Garlic can be mulched when the plants are six to eight inches high. Use a fine mulch like hulls, grass clippings, or chopped leaves. See "onions".

Grapes   See the chapter on perennial plants.

Kale   Kale is an incredibly hardy vegetable. It can be grown nearly any time of year. A fall or winter crop may be left in the field, covered lightly with something like salt hay, pea or cranberry vines or straw. Later in the winter remove the snow—one of the mulches kale seems to like best, by the way—and cut the leaves as you want them. Kale will sometimes keep this way all winter, if it doesn't get smothered by ice after a thaw.

Leeks   Leeks and scallions can be mulched lightly with anything from straw to wood shavings. Just be sure that the mulch does not interfere with the very young seedlings. See "onions".

Lettuce   *Leaf lettuce* does well in semi-shade and in humus-rich soil. A very coarse mulch such as twigs, rye straw or even pine boughs can be used in the seedbed. As the leaves grow, move the mulch right up underneath them. This does four things: it holds the soil moisture, keeps the leaves from being splashed with mud, prevents rot, and maintains the cool root run that many plants—especially cool-season vegetables like this—require for optimum production.

You can apply as much as three inches of mulch whenever *head lettuce* is three or four inches high and has started to send out its leaves. According to Arthur Burrage, this helps to insure good plant growth. Every head should mature properly this way. Burrage says, "It has always been a pleasure to look at the lettuce bed. There are rows of perfect heads resting on a light brown carpet of delightful appearance."

Melons   (See cantaloupes or watermelon)

Onions   Mulching helps onions. Almost everyone seems to agree on that. Even our man Dick Raymond, who is hesitant to mulch many things because he understands Vermont's fickle climate so well, remarks, "You can't kill an onion." He says they can be mulched during long hot spells. Chopped leaves can be sprinkled among the green shoots even if they are two or three inches high. Mulched onions should grow slowly and more succulent than ones grown without it. A little more mulch can be added as the tops develop.

Ruth Stout, who Dick Raymond opposes more often than not, says,

> Onion sets may be just scattered around on last year's mulch, then covered with a few inches of loose hay; by this method you can "plant" a pound of them in a few minutes, and you may do it, if you like, before the ground thaws.

Arthur Burrage uses a slightly modified approach. He puts down two to four inches of mulch whenever the onion tops are about six inches high. He says,

> For this mulch we use the remnants of what mulch was used in the bean, corn and pea area of the previous year. We find that the remnants are broken down into smaller pieces and are easier to handle in rows planted close together than something like fresh straw. The few weeds that grow are easily pulled and the beds stay neat looking all summer. Our experience has been that our troubles, at least as far as onions are concerned, are over for the season. Nothing is left to do except to pick them.[61]

I planted onion sets in three ways this year. (1) I planted them in bare ground and left them alone. (2) I planted them in bare ground and mulched them with finely chopped leaves when they were four to six inches high (this looks most attractive incidentally). (3) I threw—did not plant—onion sets under about six inches of hay mulch. I notice that the growth of the onions in bare ground has been very slow. And it almost seems that those mulched with the chopped leaves have stopped growing entirely. But the ones under hay have done well, growing large bottoms. Explain that one to me if you can.

Parsley In places where winter is not as harsh as in Vermont, parsley can be protected by mulch throughout the winter. It can be planted in cold frames in August—or even later—covered with hay, left in the frames all winter and transplanted to the garden in the early spring.

Parsnips will store well in winter under a heap of leaves or other protective mulch.

Parsnips   Parsnips do not grow well in tight, compacted soil. Instead of growing one straight root, they divide into three or four, which makes the root worthless. Mulching can help here by preventing compaction. But they want a soil with a pH of about 6.5, so don't use an acid mulch. Parsnips, like beets, will suffer if there is boron deficiency in your soil. Seaweed, again, has traces of boron and is often recommended for winter protection. Try some on your parsnips.

Last winter I had the misfortune to ski on a *very* cold day in January. The temperature at the top of nearby Mt. Mansfield was about -30 degrees F. with a high wind. An abominable snowman helped me off the chairlift at the top of the otherwise-abandoned mountain. When he spoke through his frosty whiskers, I recognized him as a friendly, life-long resident of Stowe Village, six miles below. "Think this cold'll hurt the parsnips?" he asked. I allowed as how I wasn't sure.

Vermonters eat parsnips from their gardens all winter. They are heaped high with leaves or some other protective mulch as cold weather moves in. They store very well under there. Don't use them until after the first heavy frost, they won't have reached their peak of quality until then anyway. Most folks think they are best in November and December. Will they survive minus thirty degrees? I keep forgetting to ask my mountain-top friend how his fared.

Peas will grow through a light straw mulch. As the plants get started, increase the mulch to insulate the soil from the heat of the sun. This way you are almost assured of a cool, moist root run.

Peas It is easy to overdo mulching peas in a cool climate like ours. The soil around peas *does* need to be cool and damp. In dry soil they will not germinate well and a large percentage of the seeds will be lost. In late spring around here, we usually don't have any trouble meeting either of these conditions without using mulch.

To grow peas in much warmer places—or to grow pea varieties like "Wando" later in the summer—mulch with a thin layer of grass clippings, straw or hay when the seeds are sown. (We broadcast peas in some places and then bury them just under the surface with the roto-tiller). As the plants get started, you can increase the mulch to insulate the soil from the atmosphere and the hot sun. This way you can almost assure yourself of a cool, moist root run.

On the sixth of June this year, just as I was finishing planting my own peas in the traditional way—in rows without mulch—my wife called me to lunch. I still had a large fistful of seeds in my hand. Indolent fellow that I am, (also very hungry at that point, and a *little* curious too if the truth be known), I more or less threw the seeds away instead of putting them carefully back in the bag. In what was a furtive sweeping gesture I quickly tossed the evidence of my own wastefulness under the rug of very heavy hay mulch. To my surprise, even though they actually were never planted in the soil, they came up *en masse* and look healthy and green.

We broadcast the same variety (Little Marvel) in a rather shady section of one of our test gardens, tilled them under, and covered them with winter rye which we just had cut from another section of the garden. The results *there* were very disappointing. So few plants came up that Dick's comment was that "they weren't even neighbors!" What the problem was, we are not sure.

The last time you pick your peas, each season, pull up the whole vine before you remove the pods. This should help save your back. The vines should be stacked and saved too. Chopped or whole, they are a nitrogen rich mulch which should be used anywhere on the garden, except on other peas.

Peppers The growing habits of sweet peppers are very much like those of tomatoes. We often plant these two at the same time as "companion" plants. Early plants respond well to a felt paper mulch. This will collect the heat of the day and help maintain a warm soil temperature for a while into the night. Later the tar paper can be taken off and replaced with an organic mulch, or not replaced at all.

I have learned that pepper plants grown under hay mulch may be stunted and slow to mature. On the other hand, my own pepper plants which are surrounded with dark, chopped leaf mold mixed with alfalfa meal, are quite a bit ahead of some of the peppers in our test gardens. Peppers and dark-colored mulches seem to go well together.

Potatoes Potatoes, if you use mulch, don't even need to be planted! As Ruth Stout says,

> Many people have discovered that they can lay seed potatoes on last year's mulch, or on the ground or even on sod, cover them with about a foot of loose hay, and later simply pull back the mulch and pick up the new potatoes.

This oversimplification may be what some would consider another unfortunate Stoutism, but you *can*

Mulch seems to thwart the potato bug. In our test garden the potato plants around the edges of the mulched plot were badly eaten by the bugs. The ones in the middle had few bugs—some of which were not potato bugs.

grow potatoes "under mulch, in mulch, on top of mulch—almost any way in fact—and get satisfactory results." You can harvest early potatoes from their thick mulch bed, and then replace the covering.

Our test garden at Dick Raymond's home, has had a potato bug problem this year. We have been after them with rotenone. Most of the potatoes were planted in furrowed rows without any mulch. But one small patch consists of potatoes that were thrown on top of the ground under eight or ten inches of mulch—à la Ruth Stout. The plants around the edges of the patch are pretty badly eaten by the bugs. The ones in the middle have a few bugs, (some of which are *not* potato bugs), but there are nowhere near as many as those along the outer perimeter. So deep mulch seems to thwart the potato bug whose egg winters in the soil. Apparently these fellows are reluctant to climb up the potato stem through the thick hay.

Pumpkins Pumpkins will profit from new-cut hay, composted leaves, straw and cow manure. Mulch around each hill. Any coarse mulch which keeps the fruit off the ground and clean can be used as the crop starts to mature.

Raspberries See the chapter on perennial plants.

Rhubarb See chapter on perennial plants.

Rutabaga (See beets)

Spinach Mulching spinach and similar vegetables such as Swiss Chard, seems like a waste of time to us, but some say that it can be mulched with grass clippings, chopped hay or ground corn cobs and be better for it. Since spinach does not do well in acid soil, avoid peat moss, oak and beech leaves, pine needles and some kinds of sawdust. In any case, we don't advise putting down a summer mulch until after the leaves have had a chance to make a good growth.

Squash Squash can use an "extra special dose of mulch", especially during hot dry spells. The mulch, whether it be rotted sawdust, compost, hay, or just leaves, can be as deep as four inches. Leave the center open so that some heat can get to the middle of the

Mulch in a squash patch will preserve moisture and discourage some bugs. Leave the center open so some heat can get to the middle of the plant.

plant. The mulch over the rest of the patch will preserve moisture and discourage some bugs. I probably don't need to remind you about how much space is taken up by squash. Be sure that you have *plenty* of mulch before you commit yourself. Don't bother mulching winter squash.

Kerr Sparks, a friend of mine, grows beautiful zucchini and acorn squash in a rock mulch—and I mean *rocks*, not crushed stone. Some of the rocks are ten to twelve inches in diameter. His wife and some of his neighbors started worrying about his sanity when he started packing these big stones around his young squash plants. "They didn't do much at first," he says, "but later in the spring when the sun got to the rocks, it was frightening. The plants grew as much as seven inches in a day!"

He gave me one huge zucchini to try. It was every bit as tender as the young, small zucchini I normally prefer. And the seeds, for some reason, were small, few and far between. This must have something to do with the fast growth the squash makes as it rests on the warm stones. Do you have a lot of rocks around your place you don't know what to do with?

Strawberries   See the chapter on perennial plants.

Sweet potatoes   Sweet potatoes are ravenous feeders and are happiest in plenty of moisture. Compost is an ideal mulch for just these reasons. Old leaves and grass clippings make a good organic side-dressing as do the old standbys, hay and straw. If you plant sweet potatoes in hills, mulch them well, fertilize them well, and allow lots of room for them to develop.

Tomatoes   Some vegetables such as tomatoes (as well as peppers and corn) need thoroughly warmed soil to encourage ideal growth. A mulch that is applied too early in the spring, before soil temperatures have had a chance to climb a little in frost zone areas, will slow such crops. Generally, in colder climates like ours, tomatoes need less mulch. Dark-colored mulches can help seal heat and moisture in.

A good *time* to mulch is right after the flowers appear. Blossom-end rot can be caused by a variable moisture supply. Mulch keeps a more consistent supply of moisture around the roots of the plants. We have used many different things: chopped alfalfa hay, chopped pea vines, chopped leaves and straw. Early plantings have been mulched with tar paper. If you find that you have lots of mulch and few sticks to use as tomato stakes, forget about staking. Let your plants run around freely over the mulch and let the fruit ripen there.

Turnips   (See beets)

Watermelon   Here is still another plant that should not be mulched until the soil is really warm. How many gallons of water do you suppose there are in one large watermelon? Obviously they demand all kinds of soil moisture. The best time to apply mulch is when the soil has been dampened thoroughly. Up to six inches of mulch can be spread over the entire patch, if you like, to prevent rot and to keep the fruit dirt-free.

The next chapter is an informal case history (with pictures) of the summer of 1952—a time when a drought meant disaster for many home gardeners in this area. It is a story of how one flexible and creative group of gardeners not only survived, but prospered in their work. They invented nothing new that season as far as I can tell, and their tale is hardly the great adventure story of all time, but they kept a careful and valuable record of their success, and have a great deal to teach us.

[8]

here's how it all began

Nineteen-fifty-two was a pretty dry summer here in Vermont. It rained some in April, May and June, but then it seemed to quit! The Weather Bureau in Burlington, fifteen miles away, reported an only *slightly* below normal precipitation level for the month of August. But down next to Lake Champlain in Charlotte, it hardly rained at all. In fact, there were seven weeks with *no* significant amount of rainfall.

There was no way anyone could have predicted this drought, of course, but a group of experimental gardeners, working in what turned out to be our original Vermont test garden, was able to do something about it—almost without planning to.

Their story, simple as it is, was one of the Genesis chapters in The Garden Way movement. No one of that small group possibly could have foreseen—just as they could not foresee the drought—that in twenty years Garden Way Associates would consist of eight different companies which together would employ nearly five hundred people. Who could have known then that Garden Way in two decades would be having a serious impact on the attitudes, gardening procedures and lifestyles of millions of people throughout the United States and around the world?

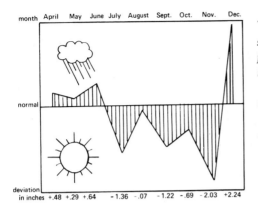

This simplified graph shows the departure from normal precipitation during part of 1952. These figures were recorded by the United States Weather Service in Burlington, fifteen miles from Garden Way's first test garden.

"You know," Lyman Wood said over a relaxed lunch at his Charlotte home the other day, "Garden Way activity has been going on here in Charlotte only since 1951." Lyman is the incredibly busy head of all of Garden Way, but when the subject of gardening comes up he always seems to have time to sit down and talk. "We used to call it Home, Farm and Garden Research . . . We've learned a lot about gardening here."

Lyman and his family, along with Ed and Carolyn Robinson—authors of the Have-More Plan, a famous series of books and pamphlets published at the end of the Depression and in the early Forties and which dealt with all aspects of homesteading and self-sufficient country living—were looking for answers.

Even in 1952 as they were looking for solutions to big philosophical questions, the first strains of the Garden Way theme could be heard: Isn't the concept of a *greener, happier more peaceful world* really within the realm of possibility? *Can't* people be taught that many environmental, economic and social ills can be alleviated if more families would be less dependent on the system as it is, and grow more of their own food in vegetable and fruit gardens?

Together with Ed Paquin, the hired man, and Alva Carpenter, a blacksmith from down the road in North Ferrisburg, who was helping them develop new gardening tools and machinery, they *also* were looking for answers to little practical questions like: What happens when you plant things through mulch?

"It was *hot* that summer!" Lyman recalled. "I remember we were playing around a lot with mulch. And planting through mulch. It was sort of a new idea then, though I guess Ruth Stout must have been doing a lot with it. We didn't know about her yet. It's funny it turned out to be such a *dry* year. Because of the drought, we were able to prove a lot more to ourselves than we thought we would."

"What *did* you prove?"

"Well, for one thing, if you want to plant in the middle of a summer like that one, you can't do it without mulch. You just can't hold the moisture. Nothing will germinate. As the dry summer went on, we found ourselves trying to see if we could get the garden to *continue* to germinate. In most situations the first planting is usually okay in the spring. The soil is damp enough. No problem without mulch. But if you want to continue planting through the summer, either for another quick crop of peas or beans, or for growing fall vegetables, you just aren't going to get the germination unless you hold the moisture.

"We proved, at least we thought we did, that mulch was not only one answer to the no-moisture problem—and we didn't fudge this, you know, by running water under the mulch or anything; nothing got watered—but that mulching was a way of gardening without having to weed or cultivate."

I showed Lyman some old photographs from his own complete files. They were twenty-one years old—all carefully dated and annotated.

"Nothing out of date about these," he said. "You ought to use some of these in your book."

"I will," I said. "If you can remember anything about them."

That must have sounded like a challenge. Here then are a few of the pictures and just some of what Lyman could "remember" about them:

Here we see a good heavy mulch between rows of strawberries. By "good and heavy" I mean three to four inches of hay, the way it comes in layers from bales. I see this picture was taken June 27, 1952, about six weeks after this mulch was applied. See how there are no weeds? The hay was partially decomposed when we put it on, because it was left baled in the field since the summer before. At this point it was easy to part with a pitchfork.

Here we are using a pointed hoe to make a new seed row between rows of strawberries. As you can see, the soil is moist and crumbly where the mulch has been parted. This soil had been tilled with a roto-tiller about two months before, when these strawberry plants were set out.

If it had not been for the mulch, there probably would have been lots of weeds growing here. The soil would have been fairly hard. We would have had to dig and till again. But because the mulch was there, it was easy to make the seed row with this hoe.

This is my daughter, Nancy, pulling mulch back away from the string to make another seed row. The ground under the mulch was so moist that her knee is damp from where she has been kneeling. The tool she is using was made by Alva Carpenter from a large spike. I still have it around somewhere. It is one of the handiest tools I have, especially for weeding. Here in the mulch, of course, we had to do very little of that.

Depending on the state of fertility of your soil, you may or may not have to put on fertilizer when you plant. We did apply it in this case after string beans had been planted, covered, and the row tramped down. I think we used one can of 5-10-5 fertilizer to a fifty foot row. The row was then left exposed until the plants got a good start. Today I suppose Dick Raymond would object to this. He might worry about burning the seed and would probably use some organic fertilizer instead. We got away with it anyway.

This picture was taken nine days later. The beans measured five inches on the ruler. There had been no rain, according to my notes. No watering was done. Without the mulch and without rain, it might have been another week or so before they would have progressed this far.

Notice that still there are no weeds. If the mulch had not been there to begin with, we would have to cultivate at least once and probably twice before the beans would have reached a height where they could be mulched in the usual way without danger of covering them or damaging them. I see that you have grown beans from seeds that were covered with mulch from the beginning. I don't think we tried that.

This picture was taken July 14th—that's seventeen days after planting—and still no rain! Now the beans were eleven inches high. We were right in the middle of the seven weeks drought here in Charlotte. Notice that still there are no weeds.

This picture was taken August 18th, fifty-two days after planting. This variety of beans, "Bountiful" as I recall, regularly matures under normal conditions in forty-five to fifty days. The mulch has brought this crop through practically on schedule in spite of no rain at all until three days before this picture was taken.

Note that still there are no weeds. No cultivating or weeding whatever was done. The only work in raising this row of beans was in the original mulching—not much work at all—and in planting—hardly more than if there had been no mulching. Also notice that there is a complete absence of disease or insect damage to the bean plants. No spraying or dusting of any kind was done. And according to the various neighbors and friends who had beans from this row, no tastier beans ever have been eaten.

This shows a tomato transplanted with practically no set-back in spite of the prevailing dry weather. The mulch has continued to keep the soil moist, providing an ample supply of moisture for the plant to take hold and keep going—without watering at all.

This is a pepper transplant that also got a good start without watering or set-back. It was a simple thing to push the mulch back and make room for the plant. If we had transplanted it before we mulched, it would have been hard to get so much mulch so close to the plant without damaging it.

This lettuce was planted on July 15th in the midst of the drought. The mulch was pulled away and the seeds were planted. The picture was taken August 18th—thirty-five days later.

These peas were planted the same day, July 15th, in the midst of the drought. The picture, like the last, was taken August 18th. A fine crop of peas was harvested from these vines early in September. This illustrated to us that mulching can shorten your growing time with certain crops. Without mulching **before** planting, the peas would have been so slow in germinating that they might have had little or no chance of maturing if we had had an early frost that year.

The corn shown here was planted July 15th in soil that had been mulched since the beginning of the season. Remember that there was no watering or irrigation of any kind. The note tells me that this was the "Gold Mine" variety, which normally matures in fifty-five or sixty days, which it did in spite of the drought. This picture was taken on the 25th of September.

Here is another way to plant after mulching. The hay, which we originally applied in layers from bales, was pushed aside in "blocks". The seeds were laid on the surface of the soil and compost was filled in over them and packed down. This provided a very fertile environment for the seeds. The hay kept the compost in place, and since it was second-cut hay, practically free of weed seeds, no hand weeding had to be done. This method of using compost makes it go a long way, gives the seeds an extra good start, and eliminates the necessity of making a seed row with a hoe.

This picture is dated October 1, 1952. Ed Paquin has just transplanted a strawberry plant—on October first in Vermont!

This is Ed Robinson with the same plant. The date here is October 20th, after we had had a couple of frosts. The plant is doing well. We gave it more mulch still as the fall went on, and it was strong and healthy in the spring.

This is Ed's wife, Carolyn Robinson, replenishing and fluffing the mulch in the corn field. The photo is dated October 20th—the same day. This mulch seemed to prolong the life of the corn in spite of the chilly fall weather.

All the time he was talking, Lyman kept reminding me that mulching was good in *this particular year*, especially because of the drought, but that it might have been a very *bad* idea had it been an entirely different type of season. "Let's not give people the impression that we are permanent, year-round mulchers here. I know Dick feels strongly about this." I assured him I would remember that.

epilogue

(more unrequired reading)

It took me twenty-seven years to recover from those boringly hot days in my mother's garden and to recover some of the wonderment I see written all over my daughter's face when she looks at growing things. If anyone had told me several years ago that today I would be a "gardening freak" I would have acknowledged the prediction with a cynical chuckle.

No one—except maybe an old man in Landgrove, Vermont—could have convinced me that freshly-tilled soil is as beautiful as new snow on the top of Mt. Mansfield or that the first radish of the season is as exciting as sailing on Lake Champlain in a strong north wind. I know better now, but an earlier me would be shocked to see that man who sits motionless in the garden for long periods watching and worrying, and planning how it is going to be better next year.

It's all because an elderly writer and organic gardening authority by the name of Sam Ogden, one day when I visited him in Landgrove, sensed my conviction that I had a black thumb. "Plants aren't as fragile as you think they are," he said as he led me into his huge and immaculate garden. "Don't be afraid."

He apologized that his garden was not what it used to before his wife—a "Kentucky Wonder" as he called her—died. For me, through his bushy white mustache, he reduced man's fascination with plants to the simplest possible terms. "The real beauty of gardening," he said, "Is in the knowledge that when you plant seed in the spring something is going to happen. Germination is an annual miracle that never fails to repeat itself."

The most comforting thing about gardening is that no one, not even a life-long expert like Sam Ogden, has all the answers. I am sure that I have left many questions about mulching unanswered. But anyone who says he knows it all should be drummed out of the gardening corps—not because he is a know-it-all, but because somewhere along the line he has lost that sense of mystery, that feeling of humble uncertainty that all gardeners should have.

"The real beauty of gardening," he said, "Is in the knowledge that when you plant seed in the spring something is going to happen. Germination is an annual miracle that never fails to repeat itself."

The botanical scientists and horticultural experimenters *must* keep on with their good work. They must
continue to give us direction and reduce as much as
possible the chances of our failing with our gardens.

But happily, because there are so many, *many* vari-
ables in gardening, because it is so very difficult—if not
impossible—to duplicate tightly controlled laboratory
conditions outdoors, because all of the enemy elements
refuse to be catalogued and thwarted, it should be a
century or two before the scientists can tell us everything. Even then it is doubtful that Mother Nature will
allow herself to be regulated altogether.

So if this generation, or even the next, has trouble
distinguishing between scientific *fact* and old wives'
remedies that seem to work in the garden, no one
should worry about it too much. Once all the question
marks are erased, once all the mysteries have been
solved, gardening may not be so much fun anymore.
Keep the faith.

A few evenings ago—it must be many evenings ago
by now—my three-year-old came into the garden again,
of her own accord. She wanted to help, and I didn't
want to let her go again. And we did some simple jobs
together. We laid walkways of hay mulch between
rows of vegetables. We tucked chopped hay around
cabbage plants. Her stubby fingers did just fine. We
sprinkled chopped leaves around onion tops, and
planted more string beans under mulch. She asked
questions and I did my best to answer. Lots of times I
said, "I don't know."

And last night she was waiting outside the door to
greet me when I came home. "Come on," she said, and
took me by the hand. She led me past the pen without
even a glance at the ten puppies inside, and into the
garden. She led me expertly through a labyrinth of
walkways, avoiding places where things we couldn't
see were growing under mulch. She showed me how a
pepper with a pointed bottom was turning red. She
showed *me* where a precocious Kentucky Wonder pole
bean tendril had wound its way to the top of its pole

and beyond—Heavenward—to where its reach was already exceeding its grasp. Standing there, holding my daughter's hand, I was awe-struck and dumbfounded by the symbolism of the moment. Who says the chances for a greener, happier, more peaceful world are no good?

sources consulted

Bear, Firman E. "Effect of Wood Shavings and Sawdust on Soil." *Sawdust, Woodchips and Shavings.* U.S.D.A. (date unknown).

Burrage, Albert. *Burrage on Vegetables.* Van Nostrand, New York, 1954.

Bruning, Walter F. *Minimum Maintenance Gardening Handbook.* Harper and Row, New York, 1968.

Bush-Brown, James and Louise, *America's Garden Book.* Charles Scribner's Sons, New York, 1958.

Carlton, R. Milton. *Vegetables for Today's Gardens.* Wilshire Book Co., N. Hollywood, Cal., 1972.

Cook, Charles (ed.). "A Guide Through the Vegetable Garden." *Yard and Fruit,* vol. 1 no. 6, 1973.

Cruso, Thalassa. *Making Things Grow Outdoors.* Alfred A. Knopf, New York, 1971.

Flanagan, Ted. "Plastic Mulch." *The Green Mountain Gardener,* University of Vermont, 1969.

Foley, Daniel J. *Gardening for Beginners.* Funk and Wagnalls, 1967.

Foster, Catherine O. *The Organic Gardner.* Vintage, New York, 1972.

Foulds, Raymond, Jr. "Mulching." University of Vermont, 1973.

Harberger, Gretchen Fisher. *McCall's Garden Book.* Simon and Schuster, New York, 1968.

Hopp, Henry. *What Every Gardener Should Know About Earthworms.* Garden Way, 1973.

Hull, George F. *The Know-Nothing Gardener's Guide to Success.* Hawthorne, New York, 1969.

Hunter, Beatrice Trum. *Gardening Without Poisons.* Houghton Mifflin, Boston, 1971.

Janick, Jules. *Horticultural Science.* W. H. Freeman and Co., San Francisco, 1963, 1972.

Kiplinger, D. C., Brooks, W. M., Utzinger, J. D., Tayama, Harry K. "Mulches for Home Grounds." Ohio State, 1970.

Kramer, Jack. *Gardening and Home Landscaping.* Harper and Row, New York, 1971.

Langer, Richard W. *Grow It!* Saturday Review Press, New York, 1972.

"Mulching Vegetables: Practices and Commercial Applications." University of Illinois, 1969.

Nuese, Josephine. *The Country Garden.* Charles Scribner's Sons, New York, 1970.

Ourecky, D.K. and Tomkins, J.P. *Raspberry Growing in New York State.* Cornell, 1971.

Pendergast, Chuck. *Introduction to Organic Gardening.* Nash Publishing, Los Angeles, 1970.

Philbrick, John and Helen. *The Bug Book: Harmless Insect Controls.* 1963.

Philbrick, John and Helen. *Gardening for Health and Nutrition.* Steinerbooks, Bleuvelt, N.Y. 10913. 1971.

Rockwell, F.F. (ed.). *10,000 Garden Questions.* Doubleday, New York, 1959.

Rodale, Robert (ed.) and staff, *The Organic Way to Mulching.* Rodale Press, Emmaus, Pa., 1972.

Shutak, V.G. and Christopher, E.P. *Sawdust Mulch for Blueberries.* University of Rhode Island, 1952.

Southwick, Lawrence. *Dwarf Fruit Trees.* Garden Way, Charlotte, Vt., 1972.

Stout, Ruth. *Gardening Without Work.* Devin-Adair, Old Greenwich, Conn, 1961.

Stout, Ruth. *How to Have a Green Thumb Without an Aching Back.* Exposition Press, New York, 1968.

Stout, Ruth and Clemence, Richard, *The Ruth Stout No-Work Garden Book.* Rodale Press, Emmaus, Pa., 1971.

Southwick, Lawrence. *Dwarf Fruit Trees.* Garden Way, Charlotte, Vt., 1972.

Thies, W.H. *Growing Fruits for Home Use.* University of Mass., 1952.

Vegetable Gardening. Southern Living Books, Birmingham, Ala., 1972.

Wells, Ortho S. *Mulching with Black Plastic in the Home Garden.* University of New Hampshire, 1971.

Wickenden, Leonard. *Gardening with Nature.* Devin-Adair, Old Greenwich, Conn. 1954.

Wyman, Donald. *The Saturday Morning Gardener.* Macmillan, New York, 1962.

footnotes

1. Thanks to Robert Rodale, ed., *The Basic Book of Organic Gardening*, (Ballantine, N.Y.: 1971), and others for helping to enumerate these many advantages to mulching.
2. Gretchen Fisher Harberger, *McCall's Garden Book*, (Simon and Schuster, N.Y.: 1968), p. 3.
3. Robert Rodale, et al. © 1971 by Rodale Press, Inc. This and other references to Rodale et al. reprinted from *The Organic Way to Mulching*, by permission of Rodale Press, Inc., Emmaus, Pa. 18049.
4. Farm and Garden Research Associates, *Gardening Without Digging or Cultivating*, unpublished, p. 11.
5. This study is cited in Beatrice Trum Hunter's, *Gardening Without Poisons*, (Houghton Mifflin, Boston: 1971), pp. 56-57.
6. R. Milton Carleton, *Vegetables for Today's Gardens*, (Wilshire Book Co., N. Hollywood, Cal.,: 1972), p. 100.
7. Headings from pp. 166-7 *Minimum Maintenance Gardening Handbook* by Walter F. Bruning and the Editors of *Home Garden Magazine*, (Harper and Row, 1970).
8. Ruth Stout and Richard Clemence, *The Ruth Stout No-Work Garden Book*, Rodale Press, Emmaus, Pa. 1971, p. 2.
9. Ibid, pp. 3, 4.
10. From *How to Have a Green Thumb Without an Aching Back: A New Method of Mulch Gardening* by Ruth Stout. Copyright, 1955, by Ruth Stout. Used by permission of the publisher, Exposition Press, Inc., Jericho, N.Y. 11753.
11. *The Ruth Stout No-Work Garden Book*, p. 119.

12. Leonard Wickenden, *Gardening With Nature* (Devin-Adair, Old Greenwich, Conn.: 1954), pp. 47-48. Reprinted with the permission of the Devin-Adair Co. Italics in these paragraphs are mine, not Mr. Wickenden's.

13. Ruth Stout, *Gardening Without Work,* (Devin-Adair, Old Greenwich, Conn.: 1961), pp. 197-198.

14. D.C. Kiplinger, W.M. Brooks, J.D. Utzinger, and Harry K. Tayama, "Mulches for Home Grounds", (Ohio State, Columbus: 1970), p. 2.

15. Ed., *Vegetable Gardening,* (Southern Living Books, Birmingham, Ala.: 1972), p. 18.

16. For the complete story on earthworms see Hopp and Taff, *What Every Gardener Should Know About Earthworms,* (Garden Way, Charlotte, Vt.: 1973).

17. James and Louise Bush-Brown, *American's Gardening Book,* (Charles Scribner's Sons, N.Y.: 1958), p. 500.

18. *Vegetable Gardening,* p. 18.

19. Ibid.

20. Robert Rodale et al., p. 98.

21. Donald Wyman, *The Saturday Morning Gardener,* (Macmillan and Co., N.Y.: 1962), p. 25.

22. Kiplinger et. al., p. 3.

23. From *Horticultural Science,* Second Edition, by Jules Janick. W.H. Freeman and Company. Copyright © 1972, p. 191.

24. Josephine Nuese, *The Country Gardener,* (Charles Scribner's Sons, N.Y.: 1970), p. 44.

25. Ibid, p. 45.

26. J. and L. Bush-Brown, p. 500.

27. Rodale, et al., p. 118.

28. Ibid, p. 119.

29. From *Introduction to Organic Gardening* by Chuck Pendergast. Copyright © 1971 by Nash Publishing. Published by permission of Nash Publishing Corporation, Los Angeles.

30. Wyman, p. 20.

31. Ibid.

32. Nuese, p. 45.

33. J. and L. Bush-Brown, p. 500.

34. Dr. Pfeiffer is quoted in John and Helen Philbrick, *Gardening for Health and Nutrition,* (Steinerbooks, Blauvelt, N.Y. 10913), p. 69.

35. Rodale et al., p. 162.

36. V.G. Shutak and E.P. Christopher, "Sawdust Mulch for Blueberries," (U. of Rhode Island, Kingston: 1952), p. 17.

37. Lawrence Southwick, *Dwarf Fruit Trees For the Home Gardener,* (Garden Way, Charlotte, Vt.: 1972), pp. 72, 93. 2, 93.

38. Rodale et al., p. 188.

39. Ibid , p. 167.

40. D.K. Ourecky and J.P. Tomkins, "Raspberry Growing in New York State", (Cornell, Ithaca: 1971), p. 13.

41. Rodale et al., p. 159.
42. W.H. Thies, "Growing Fruits for Home Use", (U. Mass, Amherst; 1952), p. 4.
43. Kiplinger et al., p. 5.
44. Arno and Irene Nehrling, *Easy Gardening with Drought Resistant Plants,* (Hearthside, N.Y.: 1968), p. 92.
45. Rodale et al., pp. 60-61.
46. Catherine Osgood Foster, *The Organic Gardener,* (Vintage, N.Y.: 1972), p. 79.
47. Donald Wyman, p. 22.
48. J. and L. Bush-Brown, p. 498.
49. John and Helen Philbrick, *The Bug Book: Harmless Insect Controls* (1963), p. 128.
50. Rodale et al., pp. 76-77.
51. A. and I. Nehrling, p. 95.
52. Donald Wyman, p. 28.
53. Ortho S. Wells, "Mulching with Black Plastic in the Home Garden", (University of New Hampshire, Durham: 1971), p. 4.
54. Firman E. Bear, "Effect of Wood Shavings and Sawdust on Soil", (USDA), pp. 2-3.
55. J. and H. Philbrick, p. 124.
56. Ibid, p. 124.
57. Rodale, et al., p. 74.
58. Dr. Flanagan is also the author of a new book from Garden Way Publishing, *Growing Food and Flowers in Containers.*
59. Much of the information and phrasing in this chapter is borrowed from other sources, primarily from *The Organic Way to Mulching* by the Rodale Press and from Albert C. Burrage, *Burrage on Vegetables,* (Van Nostrand, N.Y.: 1954).
60. Rodale et al., p. 147.
61. Burrage, p. 121.

index